Leschetizky's Fundamental Principles of Piano Technique

Leschetizky's Fundamental Principles of Piano Technique

Marie Prentner

DOVER PUBLICATIONS, INC.
Mineola, New York

Bibliographical Note

This Dover edition, first published in 2005, is an unabridged republication of the work originally published by Theodore Presser, Philadelphia, 1903, under the title *Fundamental Principles of the Leschetizky Method,* as part of "The Modern Pianist" series. The running heads reflect the series title. M. de Kendler and A. Maddock translated the original German text.

International Standard Book Number: 0-486-44279-9

Manufactured in the United States of America
Dover Publications, Inc., 31 East 2nd Street, Mineola, N.Y. 11501

DEDICATED

TO

PROFESSOR THEODORE LESCHETIZKY

WITH

HONOR AND ESTEEM.

———————

HERRN PROFESSOR THEODOR LESCHETIZKY

IN VEREHRUNG GEWIDMET.

14. APRIL, 1902.

Ich bestätige hiermit, dass Fräulein Marie Prentner durch längere Zeit meine Schülerin gewesen ist und mir schon seit einer Reihe von Jahren als eine meiner besten Assistentinnen zur Seite steht. Zugleich kann ich constatiren, dass Fräulein Prentner als Klavierspielerin in der Öffentlichkeit mit bedeutendem Erfolg gewirkt hat. Als Lehrerin hat sie durch ihre gründliche Unterrichtsweise und genaue Kenntnis meiner Methode ausgezeichnete Schüler aufzuweisen, was sie sicherlich berechtigt, ihre Erfahrungen im Klavierunterricht zu veröffentlichen.

PROFESSOR THEODOR LESCHETIZKY.

TRANSLATION.

COPY OF TESTIMONIAL.

I hereby certify that Fräulein Marie Prentner was my pupil for a very considerable time, since then having for a number of years supported and aided me in my work as one of my very best assistants. At the same time I can testify that as a pianist Frl. Prentner has performed in public with unqualified success. As a teacher, owing to the thoroughness with which she instructs and her perfect acquaintance with my method, she is able to point to artist pupils, a fact which certainly justifies her in placing before the public her experiences in teaching the pianoforte.

[Signed]   PROFESSOR THEODOR LESCHETIZKY.

EDITOR'S NOTE.

It is desired in this little note to draw attention to one or two dominating points original with this method.

One of the most important of these is the almost universal placing of the fingers in contact with their keys before they strike. This is called "preparing" the fingers. The advantages from this are two-fold. It develops absolute clarity and sureness of attack and necessitates the thinking of the following note while playing the present one, a most valuable and indispensable training. One is sure of getting a satisfying tone in both *piano* and *forte*, if with the finger-joints and knuckles held unbendingly firm and solid, the key be pushed down to its lowest possible level. In both cases the same amount of strength is exerted. The difference in stroke between a *piano* tone and a *forte* tone is, that in slow tempo the key is pushed down slower in the former than in the latter.

This leads to a second point on which too much emphasis cannot be laid, that in the following method particular weight is laid on the development of all degrees of strength from *pp* to *ff*, or, in other words, all the shadings of which a pianoforte is capable.

In conclusion be it remarked that in the study of technique as well as expression all mechanical practice is to be entirely eliminated.

M. GREENEWALT.

VORWORT DES HERAUSGEBERS.

Diese kurze Bemerkung möge ganz besonders auf einige Hauptzüge aufmerksam machen, welche dieser Methode eigen sind. Einer der bedeutendsten ist: das nach Vorbereitung der Finger auf den Tasten erfolgte Anschlagen derselben. Die Vorteile hieraus sind zweifach. Erstens, es entwickelt absolute Reinheit und Sicherheit im Greifen und zwingt, an die folgende Note zu denken, während die gegenwärtige gespielt wird; dies ist eine höchst wertvolle und unerlässliche Uebung. Man kann sowohl beim *f* als auch beim *p* auf befriedigende Klangwirkung rechnen, wenn man die Fingergelenke und Knöchel absolut unbeweglich hält und die Taste so tief niederdrückt wie es möglich ist. In beiden Fällen findet derselbe Kraftaufwand statt. Der einzige Unterschied im Anschlag zwischen einem *p* und einem *f* Ton ist, dass im langsamen Tempo bei ersterem die Taste langsamer niedergedrückt wird als bei letzterem.

Dies führt uns auf den zweiten Punkt, der nicht genug hervorgehoben werden kann, nämlich, dass in der folgenden Methode besonders Gewicht auf die Entwicklung aller Stärkegrade von *pp* zu *ff* gelegt wird, oder in anderen Worten, es sollen dem Pianoforte alle Schattierungen abgewonnen werden, deren es fähig ist.

Zum Schluss sei noch bemerkt, dass sowohl beim Studium der Technik als auch beim Vortrag alles mechanische Ueben gänzlich ausgeschlossen werde.

M. GREENEWALT.

PREFACE.

The present work contains fundamental principles, coupled with practical methods of procedure for the acquiring of a technique equal to the demands of modern pianoforte playing and execution. These principles, first laid on a solid foundation by my dear mother, I have had the privilege of enriching and deepening under the tutelage of my deeply honored and esteemed teacher, Professor Theodor Leschetizky.

In the course of twelve years' work in conjunction with this great artist and teacher I have had the opportunity of still further developing my ideas and experiences, to the exposition of which this book is devoted.

This method I have tested with a very considerable number of pupils.

I am following the suggestion of both friends and pupils as well as my own long cherished intentions in undertaking an authentic and complete publication of this method of instruction accompanied by sketches and diagrams long since prepared for the purpose, aiming especially at lucidity in every respect.

In order to give a clearer idea of my meaning I have added drawings of the position of the hands and fingers, besides numerous examples in musical notation and excerpts from piano literature.

May the aim and ideal which have filled my mind govern all those who adopt this method:

The worthy rendering of the works of our great Masters in their own spirit, founded on the fullest and freest mastery of technical principles.

VORWORT.

Die vorliegende Arbeit enthält grundlegende Prinzipien und praktische Verfahrungsweisen auf dem Gebiete der Klaviertechnik und des Klaviervortrages, die ich zunächst der Anweisung meiner unvergesslichen Mutter verdanke, dann durch das weitere Studium bei meinem hochverehrten Lehrer Professor Theodor Leschetizky zu bereichern und zu vertiefen das Glück hatte.

In zwölfjähriger Mitarbeit an der Seite dieses genialen Künstlers und Lehrers hatte ich Gelegenheit, meine Ideen und Erfahrungen noch weiter zu entwickeln, und die sich daraus ergebenden Einzelheiten bilden den Gegenstand dieses Buches.

Diese Methode habe ich an einer stattlichen Schülerschar erprobt.

Ich folge ebenso der Anregung von Freunden und von Schülern, wie auch meinen eigenen längst gehegten Absichten, wenn ich, eine authentische, vollständige und nach allen Seiten hin klare Darstellung im Auge behaltend, nunmehr die seit langem in Skizzen und Entwürfen vorbereitete Veröffentlichung der oben erwähnten Lehrmethode ins Werk setze.

Hiebei habe ich, um die Anschaulichkeit zu fördern, neben zahlreichen Notenbeispielen aus dem Gebiete des spezifisch Technischen, wie aus dem der Literatur, orientierende Abbildungen der Hand- und Fingerhaltung beigefügt.

Mögen nicht nur meine Schüler, sondern auch alle jene Kunstbeflissenen, die sich dieser Lehrweise anschliessen wollen, deren mir vorschwebendes ideales Ziel an sich erproben:

Würdige Wiedergabe der Werke unserer Meister in ihrem Geiste auf Grund vollster, freiester Beherrschung aller technischen Mittel.

CONTENTS.

PART FIRST.

MEANS FOR ACQUIRING A MODERN TECHNIQUE.

PART SECOND.

ADVICE FOR MUSICAL PERFORMANCE.

INHALT.

ERSTE ABTEILUNG.

MITTEL ZUR ERLANGUNG DER MODERNEN TECHNIK.

ZWEITE ABTEILUNG.

RATSCHLÄGE FÜR DEN MUSIKALISCHEN VORTRAG.

PREFACE TO LATEST EDITION.

From the many editions of the present work since its first appearance, I see with pleasure that it has earned numerous friends and adherents, and a very wide circulation not only in public music schools but also in private life. As I already mentioned in the preface to the first edition, this work contains fundamental principles, coupled with practical methods of procedure for the acquirement of a technic equal to the demands of modern pianoforte playing and execution, which I first received from my dear mother (school of Pirkert-Czerny) and later from my honored teacher, Prof. Theodore Leschetizky.

To the ideas and experiences which I had with the first-mentioned instructress, and in the course of the many years' work in conjunction with the great artist and teacher, Theodore Leschetizky, my own numerous ideas and experiences have been added.

I have the opportunity of testing this method each year with a very considerable number of pupils.

In order to give a clearer idea of my meaning I have added drawings of the position of the hands and fingers, besides numerous examples in musical notation and excerpts from piano literature.

May this work continue its successful course in the future also; and may those who have been interested, and who may yet become so in these studies, be guided by them in the aims and ideals, which I had in my mind:

"The worthy rendering of the great works of our immortal masters in their own spirit and feeling, founded on the fullest and freest mastery of technical principles."

VORWORT ZUR NEUESTEN AUFLAGE.

An den vielfachen Auflagen, welche das vorliegende Werk seit seinem ersten Erscheinen zu verzeichnen hat, ersehe ich mit Freude, dass es zahlreiche Freunde und Anhänger erworben und eine überaus grosse Verbreitung sowohl an den öffentlichen Musikanstalten als auch im Privatunterrichte gefunden hat.

Wie ich schon im Vorwort der ersten Auflage erwähnte, enthält diese Arbeit grundlegende Principien und praktische Verfahrungsweisen auf dem Gebiete der Klaviertechnik und des Klaviervortrages, die mir zunächst durch die Anweisung meiner unvergesslichen Mutter (Schule Pirkert-Czerny), dann durch das weitere Studium bei meinem verehrten Lehrer, Prof. Theodor Leschetizky, zu Teil wurden.

Den Ideen und Erfahrungen, die ich sowohl dem erstgenannten Unterrichte als auch der langjährigen Mitarbeit an der Seite des grossen Künstlers und Lehrers, Theodor Leschetizky, verdanke, gesellten sich meine zahlreichen eigenen.

Diese Unterrichtsweise an einer stattlichen Schülerschar zu erproben, habe ich alljährlich Gelegenheit.

Um die Anschaulichkeit des Werkes zu fördern, befinden sich neben zahlreichen Notenbeispielen aus dem Gebiete des specifisch Technischen wie aus dem der Literatur orientierende Abbildungen der Hand- und Fingerhaltung.

Möge dieses Werk seinen erfolgreichen Weg auch in Zukunft fortsetzen und Alle, die sich demselben bereits zugewendet haben und noch zuwenden werden, dem mir vorschwebenden idealen Ziele zuführen:

"Würdige Wiedergabe der grossen Werke unserer unsterblichen Meister in deren Geiste und Gefühlsleben auf Grund vollster, freiester Beherrschung aller technischen Mittel."

INTRODUCTION.

Patience and exactitude are the main conditions for success in the method herein explained. It will be far more easy for a beginner to acquire the instructions of this book than for those who have hitherto followed the rules of another method. For this reason I strongly advise the latter to give up entirely, for a time at least, the playing of pieces and sight reading, as the accustomed position and movement of the hand will be a great hindrance to the rapid adoption of a new method. The pleasure of hearing good music in the opera or concert halls during this time must compensate the pupil for the musical abstinence, which is to be persevered in until he feels that his fingers have become quite lissome and flexible.

The difference in the conformation of hands will make more necessary the close study of one chapter than of another. For instance: a small hand, scarcely able to span a seventh, will, after careful and consistent labor, be able to span a ninth, sometimes even a tenth. For this particular case patient attention must be paid to the exercises intended for the purpose,—in Chapter IX,—and this idea of bearing the individual constantly in mind must always run like a thread throughout the study of the entire method. A hand with clumsy fingers will be obliged to make greater use of the Non-legato (see Chap. II b) while, for one with fingers more loosely jointed, the Legato exercises present the greater difficulty (see Chap. II a).

It is possible by means of judicious practice to give strength to a weak hand and elasticity to a stiff one.

Naturally one is to be warned against too much practice, especially in the beginning of study. At first, in order to avoid fatiguing the muscles, the shortest time of practice is most strongly recommended, a quarter of an hour for each hand being sufficient. After going through the exercises with each hand separately the student should take a long rest, repeating the half hour's practice three or four times throughout the day. Only by degrees, as the muscles increase in strength and power of endurance, should the student increase the length of practice at a sitting. At first all the examples are to be performed with each hand separately, in order better to concentrate the full attention on the subject-matter in hand. Later the scales, arpeggios, etc., may be played with both hands together.

EINLEITUNG.

Geduld und Genauigkeit sind die ersten Bedingungen für den Erfolg der vorliegenden Lehre. Dem Anfänger wird die Aneignung des in diesem Buche *Gebotenen* entschieden leichter fallen, als dem in einer anderen Methode bereits unterrichteten Spieler. Letzterem empfehle ich vor allem das Spielen von Stücken sowie das Blattlesen für einige Zeit zu unterlassen, da die gewohnten früheren Handbewegungen der raschen Aneignung der neuen hinderlich wären. Der Genuss schöner Musik in Konzerten und Oper entschädige für die eigene musikalische Fastenzeit, welche so lange währe, bis man sich im sicheren Besitz modulationsfähiger und richtig beweglicher Finger fühle.

Der verschiedene Bau der Hände wird natürlich Veranlassung geben, dieses oder jenes Kapitel noch besonders in Anspruch zu nehmen. Bei einer kleinen Hand z. B., welche kaum eine Septime zu spannen vermag, ist bei konsequenter und vorsichtiger Arbeit die Spannung der None, in vielen Fällen sogar der Dezime erreichbar. Hier muss natürlich das Hauptaugenmerk auf die diesbezüglichen Uebungen (Kap. IX) gerichtet sein, und das planmässige Vorgehen nach diesen wird immer die allgemeine Verarbeitung des Stoffes wie ein Leitmotiv durchziehen. Eine Hand mit schwerfälligen Fingern wird mehr das Nonlegato (*siehe Kap. II.b.*) anwenden müssen, während für eine mit loser gebauten Fingern, denen die Entwicklung des Legato Schwierigkeiten bereitet, *Kap. II.a.* das Wichtigste ist. Auch einer schwachen Hand zur Kraft zu verhelfen, einer steifen, Elasticität zu verleihen, ist durch verständiges Ueben möglich.

Natürlich warne ich dabei vor Uebertreibung, besonders im Beginne des Studiums. Anfangs ist, um die Ermüdung der Muskeln zu vermeiden, die kürzeste Uebungszeit die empfehlenswerteste. Eine Viertelstunde für je eine Hand genügt. Nach Absolvierung der beiden Hände hintereinander mache man eine längere Pause und wiederhole die halbstündige Uebungszeit noch drei- bis viermal im Tage. Erst nach und nach mit der wachsenden Muskelkraft und Ausdauer steigere man auch die Dauer des Uebens.

Sämtliche Beispiele sind anfangs mit jeder Hand allein auszuführen, um die volle Aufmerksamkeit auf diese konzentrieren zu können. Erst später werden Skalen, Arpeggien u. s. w. mit beiden Händen gleichzeitig gespielt.

INTRODUCTION.

After carrying out the entire series of exercises, the following works may be found useful:

Czerny: Op. 740: The Art of Finger Dexterity (6 books).

Czerny: Op. 399: School of the Left Hand.

Czerny: Op. 337: 40 Daily Exercises.

Kullak: Op. 48: School of Octave Playing (3 books).

Tausig-Ehrlich: Daily Studies (3 books).

Clementi: Gradus ad Parnassum.

Equally as great attention must be paid to the study of Part II, dealing with musical interpretation, as to that devoted to technique. The advanced performer who, knowing his technical deficiencies, boldly determines to undertake the re-modeling of his hand, will find himself in a very short time richly repaid for his trouble. During this time the performing of works already studied cannot be recommended, for the obvious reason that a new style of playing with all its rules and laws must first become a part of the student's very personality. Old habits cannot then upset or endanger the newly erected structure.

EINLEITUNG.

Nach Durchführung der in der Folge verzeichneten Uebungen werden als Studienwerke angereiht:

Czerny: Op. 740, Kunst der Fingerfertigkeit, (6 Hefte)

Czerny: Op. 399, Schule der linken Hand.

Czerny: Op. 337, 40 tägliche Uebungen.

Kullak: Op. 48, Schule des Oktavenspieles (3 Hefte).

Tausig-Ehrlich: Tägliche Studien (3 Hefte).

Clementi: Gradus ad Parnassum.

Was das darauf folgende Studium des Vortrages anbelangt, dem ebenso grosse Aufmerksamkeit wie dem der Technik zugewendet werden muss, so sei dem avancierten Spieler, welcher sich, technischer Mängel bewusst, mutig entschlossen hat, eine Umarbeitung seiner Hand zu unternehmen, die frohe Aussicht eröffnet, dass ihn nach einer kurzen doch die Mühe reichlich lohnenden Zeit der Ueberwindung, die an die Stufe seines musikalischen Könnens anschliessende würdige Weiterentwicklung erwarte. Die Wiederholung bereits studierter Werke ist anfangs nicht empfehlenswert; erst muss die neue Spielweise mit all ihren Regeln und Gesetzen ein Teil seines Ichs geworden sein, so dass auch alte Erinnerungen den neuen Aufbau nicht erschüttern, das erstandene Gebäude nicht zerstören können.

THE MODERN PIANIST.

PART I.

MEANS FOR ACQUIRING A MODERN TECHNIQUE.

CHAPTER I.

POSITION OF THE HAND AND FINGERS.

Right Hand.

One should sit in a straight but easy attitude in front of the keyboard,—not too high,—so that the wrist can be easily bent downward.

Fig. 2 shows the correct position of the hand and fingers, to be gained in the following manner:

Position I.

Lift up (Fig. 1) the note E, two-lined octave, as

DER MODERNE PIANIST.

ERSTE ABTEILUNG.

MITTEL ZUR ERLANGUNG DER MODERNEN TECHNIK.

KAPITEL I.

DIE AUFSTELLUNG DER HAND UND FINGER.

Rechte Hand.

Man setze sich in gerader jedoch ungezwungener Haltung vor die Klaviatur; nicht zu hoch, damit das Handgelenk leicht gesenkt sei.

Fig. 2 zeigt die richtige Hand- und Fingerstellung, welche auf folgende Weise zu erreichen ist:

1. Stellung.

Man hebe (Fig. 1) die Taste E der zweigestrichenen

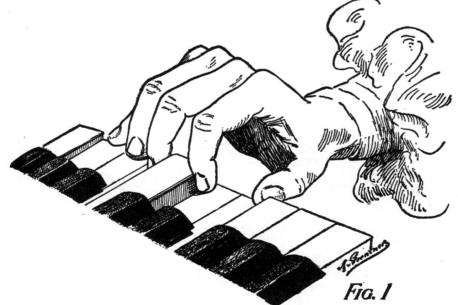

Position of the Hand and Fingers with raised note.

Hand- und Fingerstellung bei erhobener Taste.

Fig. 1

far as possible above the surface of the keyboard. The 2d and 3d * fingers, parallel with the keys and in a well-curved position, hold the note E thus raised between them. These fingers are then to be placed

***German fingering throughout.**

Oktave so weit als möglich über die Klaviaturfläche empor. Der 2. und 3. Finger umklammern in gerader Richtung der Tasten und in schön gebogener Haltung die aufgezogene Taste E. Die Finger sind fest am

firmly on the outside edges of the notes D and F, and perpendicular to them. Thus the 4th finger rests upon G, parallel to the 2d and 3d fingers, a position which will be found difficult because of the inherent tendency of that finger to bend outward. The left hand may be used to place it in the correct position. The 5th finger is to be placed upon the note A either slightly curved or somewhat stretched out, according to the individual's hand. Finally the thumb presses the note C with its extreme point. The joint of the thumb is neither to be extended too much nor contracted. The knuckles are to be held so high, that a hollow is formed between the thumb and the 2d finger, large enough for the insertion of three fingers' breadth of the unused hand, while at the same time the wrist is kept at a height equal to that of the elbow, the forearm being on a level with the keys.

The strength needed for holding the notes is to be produced without pressure of the arm, and should cause neither pain nor strain to be felt in it. The position of the fingers and thumb on the notes C, D, F, G, A (see Fig. 1, position 1) causing a separation of the 2d and 3d fingers by means of the raised note E, tends to loosen the firmly connected knuckles, and is therefore to be quietly persisted in for a time. After this the pupil changes to position II. This is done by pressing down the raised note E with the 3d finger, thus liberating the note F, which then separates the 3d and 4th fingers. This position effects the loosening of the joint which is the most tightly knit of all. After continuing to hold position II for a time, shift the 4th finger to F (G raised), which gives position III; this is followed by the 5th finger on G, position IV.

In this way the hand becomes accustomed to the position given in Fig. 2, which represents the proper disposal of the fingers.

DER MODERNE PIANIST.

äussersten Rande der Tasten D und F senkrecht zu denselben aufzustellen. Nun kommt der 4. Finger auf Taste G parallel zum 2. und 3. zu stehen, was bei seiner Neigung, sich schief nach aussen zu biegen schwierig ist. Die linke Hand kann ihm durch Zurückdrehen in die richtige Lage behilflich sein. Der 5. Finger, je nach Individualität der Hand, ist entweder leicht gebogen oder etwas gestreckt auf Taste A aufzustellen. Endlich stelle sich der Daumen auf Taste C gleichfalls mit der äussersten Spitze auf. Der Daumenknöchel werde weder zu viel herausgehalten, noch eingezogen. Während der ganzen Aufstellung sind die Mittelhandknöchel so hoch zu halten, dass sich zwischen Daumen und 2. Finger eine so grosse Wölbung bilde, dass man drei aufeinander liegende, wagrecht gehaltene Finger der anderen Hand einschieben kann. Dazu leichte Handgelenkshaltung in gleicher Höhe mit dem Ellbogen und der Armlinie, in gerader Fortsetzung der Tastenrichtung.

Die Kraft der Fingeraufstellung wird ohne Nachdruck des Armes erzeugt; es soll sich keinerlei Schmerz oder auch nur Spannung im Arme fühlbar machen. Die Stellung der fünf Finger auf C, D, F, G, A (siehe Fig. 1), also die 1. Stellung, welche eine Trennung des 2. und 3. Fingers durch die erhobene Taste E verursacht und dadurch die von Natur fest zusammenhängenden Handknöchel löst, wird eine Weile ruhig gehalten. Darauf rücke man in die 2. Stellung, indem man mit dem 3. Finger die aufgestellte Taste E niederdrückt und die Taste F emporzieht. Die jetzt zwischen dem 3. und 4. Finger aufgestellte Taste F bewirkt die Lösung des 4. Fingers, welche die schwierigste ist. Nach abermaligem Halten der 2. Stellung erfolgt das Weiterrücken des 4. auf F (aufgestellte Taste G), was die 3. Stellung bedeutet, und des 5. auf G, die 4. Stellung.

Auf diesem Wege gelangt man zu dem Vorbilde Fig. 2, womit die Hand- und Fingerstellung erledigt ist.

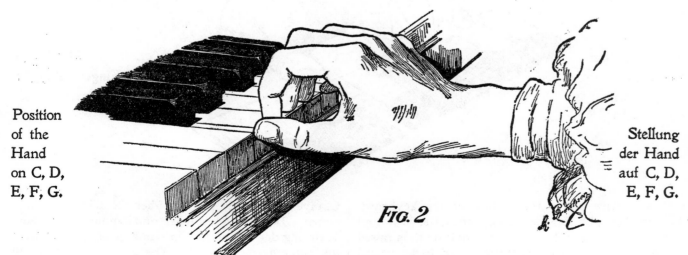

Position of the Hand on C, D, E, F, G.

FIG. 2

Stellung der Hand auf C, D, E, F, G.

Left Hand.

Position I.

The thumb on G of the small octave.
2d finger on F (E raised).
3d finger on D.
4th finger on C.
5th finger on B.

Position II.

The thumb on G.
2d finger on F.
3d finger on E (E pressed down and D raised).
4th finger on C.
5th finger on B.

Position III.

The thumb on G.
2d finger on F.
3d finger on E.
4th finger on D (D pressed down and C raised).
5th finger on B.

Position IV.

The thumb on G.
2d finger on F.
3d finger on E.
4th finger on D.
5th finger on C.

For developing an unequivocally firm grasp on the keys the following wrist exercise is given: Raise the wrist slowly, but not too high, while counting from 1 to 4; then sink it enough to touch the piano without altering the position of the fingers (see Fig. 3).

This exercise should be repeated several times between every new position taken.

Linke Hand.

1. *Stellung:*

Daumen auf G der kleinen Oktave, 2. Finger auf F (Taste E aufgehoben).
3. auf D.
4. auf C.
5. auf H.

2. *Stellung:*

Daumen auf G.
2. Finger auf F.
3. Finger auf E (Taste E wurde niedergedrückt, Taste D aufgestellt).
4. auf C.
5. auf H.

3. *Stellung:*

Daumen auf G.
2. Finger auf F.
3. Finger auf E.
4. Finger auf D (Taste D wurde niedergedrückt, Taste C aufgestellt).
5. auf H.

4. *Stellung:*

Daumen auf G.
2. Finger auf F.
3. Finger auf E.
4. Finger auf D.
5. Finger auf C.

Zur Befestigung der Fingerhaltung mache man noch folgende Handgelenksübung:

Unter Zählen von 1 bis 4 hebe man das Handgelenk langsam aufwärts, jedoch nicht zu hoch, und senke es dann so tief, dass es das Klavier berührt ohne die Haltung der Finger zu verändern (siehe Fig. 3). Mehrmalige Wiederholung dieser Uebung.

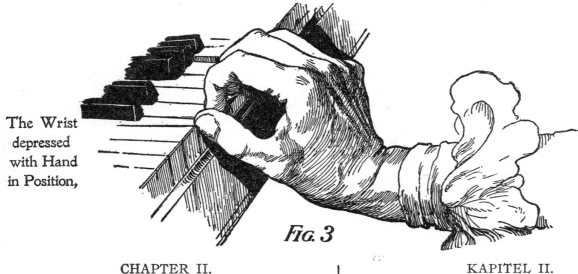

The Wrist depressed with Hand in Position,

Senkung des Handgelenkes bei unveränderter Fingerhaltung.

FIG. 3

CHAPTER II.

TOUCH.

The subject of tone production is a very extensive one. It is best classified under the following headings:

Legato.
Non-legato.
Finger Staccato.
Staccato from the Wrist (I).
Staccato from the Wrist (II).
Portamento.

With these exercises every degree of intensity in sound from *pp*, to *ff*, must be developed.

KAPITEL II.

DER ANSCHLAG.

Das Gebiet der Tonbildung ist ein sehr reiches. Man gliedert es am besten in nachstehende Hauptabschnitte:

Legato.
Non-legato.
Fingerstaccato.
Staccato aus dem Handgelenk (I).
Staccato aus dem Handgelenk (II).
Portamento.

Dabei sind gleichzeitig alle Tonstärkegrade vom *pp*, bis zum *ff*, auszubilden.

THE MODERN PIANIST.

LEGATO.

I. Preliminary Practice for Single Fingers.

Right Hand.

Example 1 *a, Position* as in Fig. 1, the keys being held firmly down.—Counting slowly up to 4 raise the thumb with the key C, from which it is not to be removed even when the key has reached its normal level, and press the note down audibly, giving an inaudible second pressure without re-raising the finger, for added exercise in strengthening the touch. This exercise is to be repeated several times.

DER MODERNE PIANIST.

LEGATO.

I. Vorübung der einzelnen Finger.

Rechte Hand.

Beispiel 1 *a.*—Aufstellung wie in Fig. 1. Die Tasten werden fest niedergehalten. Man hebt den Daumen bei sehr langsamem Zählen von 1 bis 4 gleichzeitig mit seiner Taste auf, welche, auch in die normale Höhe zurückgekehrt, von diesem nicht verlassen werden darf. Nun ist die Taste C klingend herabzudrücken, worauf zur Stärkung des Fingers ein stummer Nachdruck desselben erfolgt ohne den Finger wieder zu erheben. Man wiederhole diesen Vorgang mehrere male.

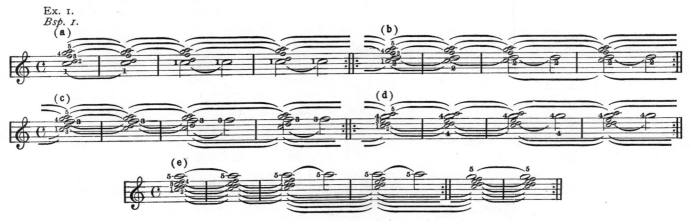

Ex. 1.
Bsp. 1.

Example 1 *b and c.*—The 2d and 3d fingers are to be drilled similarly, with the hand still in position 1 (Fig. 1). For the 4th finger (Ex. 1 *d*) the second position is necessary and for the 5th finger (Ex. 1 *e*) the third position. Practise at first *pp*, as a strain to the arm is in this way most easily avoided. All degrees of intensity from *pp* to *ff* are to be practised until a feeling of complete independence of finger is reached. The thumb, which is naturally the strongest finger, must always strike *p*, as the fineness of the touch as well as its uniformity with that of the other fingers presents, in this case, the greater difficulty. For gaining a good legato as well as flexibility of finger the following examples (2) are to be practised.

Beispiel 1 *b und c.*—In der 1. Stellung (Fig. 1) sind auch der 2. und 3. Finger in gleicher Weise vorzunehmen. Für den 4. Finger (Bsp. 1 *d*) ist die 2. Stellung und für den 5. (Bsp. 1 *e*) die 3. Stellung dazu erforderlich. Man übe zuerst *pp*, da in diesem Falle am ehesten das Anspannen der Armmuskeln zu vermeiden ist. Bis man die Empfindung der vollkommenen Unabhängigkeit des arbeitenden Fingers bekommen hat, entwickle man aus dem *pp* nach und nach alle Stärkegrade bis zum *ff*. Der Daumen, der von Natur kräftigste Finger, übe mehr *p*, da ihm die Feinheit sowie auch Gleichförmigkeit im Anschlag mit den anderen Fingern grössere Schwierigkeit bereitet. Zur Verbindung und Beweglichkeit der Finger sind folgende Beispiele (2) zu exerzieren.

Ex. 2.
Bsp. 2.

11

As in these exercises the fingers hold the keys after they have struck them, all five notes will sound together, but in spite of this dissonance the exercises, on account of their usefulness, must not be altered or omitted.

All the examples should be practised, first throughout *p* and then *f*, secondly from *pp al crescendo* to *ff* and *decrescendo* in the same way.

II. Completed Legato.

The thumb and 2d finger are to be "prepared" ready for playing, and by "prepared" is meant, throughout this work, the placing of the fingers in contact with their keys ready for their audible sounding, and not depressed. The thumb strikes C; the soundless second pressure following. Then the 2d finger strikes while the 3d is quickly "prepared" on E, the thumb at the same time leaving its key, so that the continued vibration of its note may be avoided. While the 3d finger is striking, the "preparing" of the 4th finger upon F and the simultaneous raising of the 2d finger take place. Proceed similarly with the 4th finger. On the 5th striking G, the 4th finger is again "prepared" on F, ready for playing the exercise back to C.

So by completed legato is understood the pressing down of a key by the finger already placed in contact with it ("prepared"), without its having been previously raised above the note, soundless repetition of the pressure (in slow tempo), and the raising of the finger only when the next one in order of playing has begun striking in the same manner.

It must be further remarked that in a legato five-finger exercise in slow tempo all the fingers **except the thumb** are raised fairly high after the stroke; the thumb remains constantly on or close to its key, for the sake of keeping the hand steady. In quick time the fingers are, of course, raised less, the 5th being the one always raised highest.

All the foregoing exercises in which two or more fingers come into consecutive use, are now to be repeated with a correct legato touch.

NON-LEGATO.

Right Hand.

The non-legato is made to differ in effect from the legato through the "unprepared" striking of the fingers. As a preliminary exercise take position Fig. 1, playing as follows with the thumb: Counting slowly 1 and 2, the finger rises with the key; when at the normal level of the key the finger keeps on with its upward motion while one counts 3 and 4 until it is raised as high as possible above the key. Hereupon it drops quickly from its height on to the key

Da bei diesen Uebungen die Finger auch nach dem Anschlage liegen bleiben, so tönen alle fünf Tasten in einander, was keineswegs wohlklingend ist, aber seiner Nützlichkeit halber nicht unterlassen werden kann.

Alle Beispiele sollen erstens durchwegs *p* und durchwegs *f*, zweitens vom *pp* in das *ff* crescendierend und ebenso decrescendierend geübt werden.

II. Ausgebildetes Legato.

Daumen und 2. Finger stehen vorbereitet. Unter "Vorbereitung der Finger" verstehe ich die Aufstellung derselben auf die nicht niedergedrückten Tasten. Der Daumen schlägt C an; stummer Nachdruck. Darauf Anschlag des 2. Fingers, während der 3. auf E rasch vorbereitet wird und der Daumen gleichzeitig seine Taste verlässt, damit das Weitertönen derselben abgeschnitten wird. Während der 3. anschlägt, erfolgt das Vorbereiten des 4. auf F und das gleichzeitige Aufheben des 2. Gleiches Verfahren bei dem 4. Bei dem Anschlagen des 5. auf G wird wieder der 4. auf F vorbereitet zum Zurückspielen der Uebung.

Unter ausgebildetem Legato versteht man also, dass der auf seiner Taste vorbereitete Finger dieselbe, ohne sich vorher von ihr zu erheben, niederdrückt, stumm nachdrückt (im langsamen Tempo) und sich erst erhebt wenn der nächste Finger in der gleichen Anschlagsweise einsetzt.

Noch sei bemerkt, dass in einer Legato-Fünffinger-übung bei langsamem Tempo das Aufheben aller Finger ziemlich hoch erfolgt, bis auf den Daumen; letzteres der ruhigen Handhaltung wegen. Bei schnellem Tempo erhalten die Finger natürlich weniger Hebung, die grösste der 5.

Alle früheren Beispiele, in welchen die Verbindung der Finger geübt wurde, sind jetzt mit dem richtigen Legatoanschlag zu spielen.

NON-LEGATO.

Rechte Hand.

Das Non-legato unterscheidet sich in der Klang-wirkung vom Legato durch den unvorbereiteten Anschlag der Finger. Als Vorübung nehme man wieder die Aufstellung der Hand, Fig. 1, vor und übe z. B. den Daumen folgendermassen: Er hebe sich gleichzeitig mit seiner Taste unter langsamem Zählen 1 und 2 nach aufwärts; in der normalen Höhe derselben angelangt, verlasse er sie und hebe sich unter weiterem Zählen 3 und 4 so hoch als möglich von der Taste auf.

and strikes it, an inaudible second pressure following. Repeat this exercise in touch several times in all degrees of intensity from *pp* to *ff*. The other fingers play similarly in the positions noted for them; the 2d and 3d fingers in the first position, the 4th in the second position, and the 5th in the third position.

The fingers play consecutively in the same way, one finger, not leaving its key until the next one has struck.

Examples No. 2 are here to be practised non-legato; all fingers, excepting the thumb, being raised as high as possible even in quick tempo. Only the finger exercises in triplets and sixteenths on one and the same key are to be omitted, as in these the non-legato touch must through speed become necessarily changed into a legato touch.

Darauf schlage er sofort, aus der Höhe kommend, dieselbe an; stummer Nachdruck erfolgt. Wiederholung dieser Anschlagsübung mehrere male vom *pp* alle Stärkegrade durch bis zum *ff*. Die anderen Finger thun das Gleiche in den für sie passenden Stellungen: 2. und 3. Finger in 1. Stellung, der 4. in 2. Stellung, der 5. in 3. Stellung.

In derselben Weise werden auch die Finger in einer Tonreihe gespielt; selbstverständlich verlässt keiner seine Taste vor Anschlag der nächsten.

Die Notenbeispiele Nr. 2 werden jetzt non-legato geübt; den Daumen ausgenommen, werden die Finger möglichst hoch gehoben, auch im schnellen Tempo. Nur die Uebungen des einzelnen Fingers auf ein und derselben Taste in Triolen und Sechzehntel lasse man weg, da in diesem Falle der Non-legatoanschlag in den Legatoanschlag übergehen müsste.

FINGER STACCATO.

Hand Position, Fig. 2.
Right Hand.

Example 3 *a*, *b*, *c*.—In finger staccato the finger, dropping from its raised position and instantly striking the key, as in the non-legato, must be raised from the latter before the next note is struck, while the hand as well as the wrist remains perfectly still. To attain this the preliminary exercise 3 *a*, *b*, *c* is to be practised, the pupil sometimes resting his thumb (*a*) or 5th finger (*b*) on the key to support the hand, while the other fingers play consecutively.

FINGERSTACCATO.

Aufstellung der Hand, Fig. 2.
Rechte Hand.

Beispiel 3 *a*, *b*, *c*.—Bei dem Fingerstaccato, wie bei dem Non-legato, muss der aus der Höhe herabfallende, die Taste direkt niederdrückende Finger dieselbe sogleich, noch vor Anschlag des nächsten, verlassen, während die Hand sowie das Handgelenk in vollkommener Ruhe verbleiben. Um dies zu erreichen, lasse man als Vorübung den Daumen (siehe Bsp. 3 *a*) oder den 5. Finger (siehe Bsp. 3 *b*) als Stützpunkt der Hand auf seiner Taste liegen, während die anderen Finger abwechselnd spielen.

STACCATO FROM THE WRIST (I).

Hand Position, Fig. 2.
Right Hand.

Example 4.—To practise this wrist staccato the finger stands "prepared" (placed in contact with its key), and after giving a quick stroke down, not only the finger but the whole hand is jerked upward from the wrist, dropping quickly back again, in so doing "preparing" the next finger.

STACCATO AUS DEM HANDGELENK (I).

Handstellung, Fig. 2.
Rechte Hand.

Beispiel 4.—Bei dieser Gattung des Staccato steht der spielende Finger vorbereitet auf der Taste; nachdem er diese kurz angeschlagen hat, schnellt er mit der ganzen Hand aus dem Handgelenk empor; dieselbe fällt rasch mit dem nächsten sich vorbereitenden Finger zurück, welch letzterer das Gleiche thut wie der vorige, jetzt ganz unbeteiligte.

Ex. 4.
Bsp. 4.

Example 5.—This staccato may be practised in another way by which a still greater sensitiveness of the finger tips can be attained. In this case all four fingers and thumb are "prepared," when, one finger striking as briefly as possible, the whole hand is jerked upward to fall back into its former position, each finger playing then in turn.	*Beispiel* 5.—Dieses Staccato lässt sich auch auf eine zweite Art üben, was eine besondere Feinfühligkeit der Fingerspitzen bewirkt; hier sollen sich alle fünf Finger zugleich vorbereiten und die mit dem auf das kürzeste anschlagenden Finger emporschnellende Hand so in ihre Lage zurückfallen, dass sämtliche Finger wieder auf ihren Tasten vorbereitet zu stehen kommen:
The large figures under the staff belong to the large notes and indicate the playing fingers; the small notes with small figures belong to the fingers which do not play but are held in "preparation." This rule holds in all the following examples.	Die grossen Ziffern unter dem Notensystem gehören zu den grossen Noten und bedeuten die spielenden Finger; die kleinen Notenpunkte mit den kleinen Ziffern bezeichnen die in Vorbereitung gehaltenen Finger. Die Erklärung dieser Schreibweise gilt für alle folgenden Beispiele.

Ex. 5.
Bsp. 5.

## STACCATO FROM THE WRIST (II).	## STACCATO AUS DEM HANDGELENK (II).
Right Hand.	**Rechte Hand.**
Example 6.—This staccato differs from the wrist staccato (1) in that the single finger drops as a unit with the raised hand on to the key, from a height and not "prepared," and, after striking it, is elastically jerked up from the wrist, still in company with the whole hand. This exercise should be practised with all the fingers in succession.	*Beispiel* 6.—Dieses unterscheidet sich von dem Staccato aus dem Handgelenk (I) dadurch, dass der Finger mit der emporgehobenen Hand rasch auf die Taste niederfällt und, dieselbe anschlagend, gleich wieder mit der ganzen Hand elastisch aus dem Handgelenk zurückprallt. Man übe auch diese Art in der Reihenfolge der fünf Finger.

Ex. 6.
Bsp. 6.

## PORTAMENTO.	## PORTAMENTO.
Tied staccato notes are often regarded as simple staccato notes; thus played they would greatly disturb the character of a serious piece of music, especially of an *Adagio* or *Largo*.	Die mit Bogen versehenen Staccatonoten werden häufig für blosse Staccatonoten gehalten und auch als solche behandelt, was die grösste Störung im Charakter ernster Tonstücke, namentlich eines Adagios oder Largos, hervorrufen würde.

Ex. 7.

Bsp. 7.

Example 7.—The portamento is practised in the following manner: The finger, "prepared," strikes the key while the wrist drops slowly, the finger leaving the note again with a gentle raising of the wrist. This causes the notes to sound long drawn out and yet distinctly separate.	*Beispiel* 7.—Das Portamento übt man folgendermassen: Der vorbereitete Finger schlägt an, während sich das Handgelenk langsam senkt, und verlässt die Taste bei sanfter Hebung desselben. Auf diese Weise klingen die Töne lang gezogen und doch von einander getrennt.
Every example in this chapter on Touch is to be applied to the left hand as well.	**Sämtliche Beispiele des Kapitels über den Anschlag sind auf die linke Hand zu übertragen.**

CHAPTER III.	KAPITEL III.
# THE DIATONIC SCALE.	# DIE DIATONISCHE SKALA.
## I. THE ASCENDING SCALE.	## I. DIE AUFWÄRTSGEHENDE SKALA.
(A) Passing the Thumb under the Fingers.	**(A) Das Untersetzen des Daumens.**

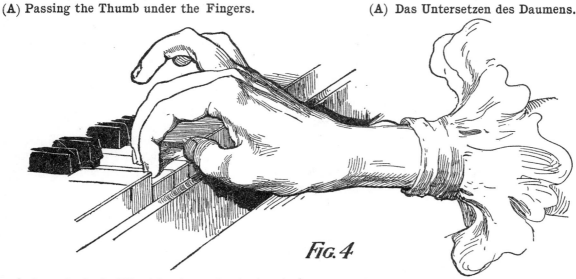

FIG. 4

One of the principal difficulties in scale-playing is the correct "passing under" of the thumb. The following thumb exercises should be practised as a preparation for scale-playing:

Eine Hauptschwierigkeit der Skala ist das richtige Untersetzen des Daumens, weshalb folgende Daumenübungen vorgenommen werden:

Ex. 8.　**Right Hand.**
*Bsp. 8.　***Rechte Hand.**

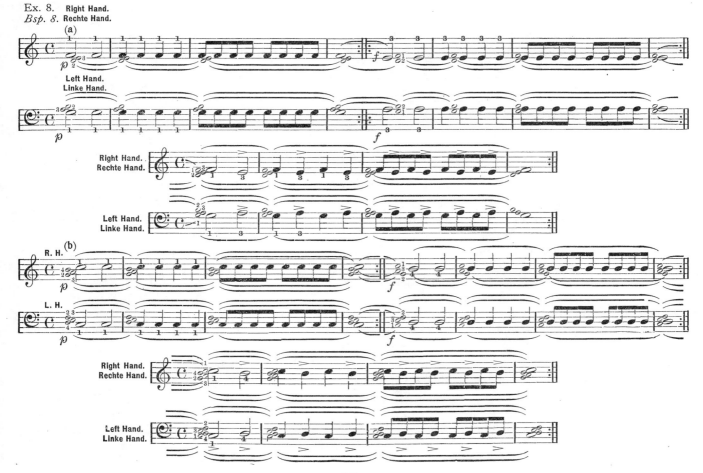

Example 8 *a*. R. H.—The 2d and 3d fingers and thumb (see Fig. 4) do not now stand in a perfectly straight line with the keys, as was hitherto the case in the five-finger exercises, but are held somewhat slanting to the keyboard by means of the elbow shifted a little to the right from the body. The 2d finger is placed almost in the center of the key, D, the 3d on E, but nearer to the black key; the thumb, which has been "passed under" on to F without disturbance of the hand position, strikes gently with its extreme point, and is gradually raised again with the key while counting slowly 1 to 4; this should be repeated several times. The 3d finger should be drilled in the same way. The thumb and 3d finger then play F and E, as if in a trill, in the slowest possible time, the 3d finger striking loudly, the thumb playing *pp*. The same exercise is to be practised with the thumb and 4th finger (Ex. 8 *b*).

Beispiel 8 *a*. R. H.—Der 2., 3. Finger und Daumen (siehe Fig. 4) stehen jetzt nicht in ganz gerader Richtung der Tasten, wie es bisher in den Fünffingerübungen der Fall war, sondern durch den ein wenig nach rechts vom Körper gehaltenen Ellbogen etwas schief zu denselben. Der 2. Finger beinahe in der Mitte der Taste D, der 3. auf E näher zur schwarzen Taste; der auf F ohne Störung der Handstellung unterlegte Daumen schlage mit seiner äussersten Spitze schwach an, erhebe sich mit der Taste unter langsamem Zählen von 1 bis 4 und wiederhole dies mehrere Male. In gleicher Weise ist der 3. zu üben. Daumen und 3. Finger spielen dann trillerartig F und E inlangsamstem Tempo, wobei der 3. laut, der Daumen *pp* anschlagen soll. Das gleiche ist auch mit Daumen und 4. Finger auszuführen (Bsp. 8 *b*).

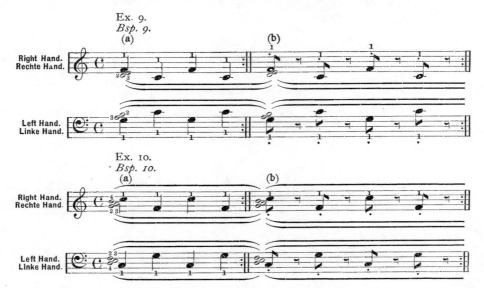

In examples 9 and 10 the position of the hand is the same as in examples 8 *a* and *b*. The thumb, always "prepared" before striking, now deftly changes its place from F to C and *vice versâ* (see Ex. 9. R. H.) without jerking the hand in the slightest. This exercise is to be practised *pp*, legato, and staccato.

Example 10 contains the same practice for the thumb, the only difference being the greater stretch from C to F, which involves greater difficulty in keeping the hand quiet.

In these exercises the knuckles are held high, the fingers well curved, the 1st and 2d joints inflexible, the wrist light, and the arm in a horizontal position.

In den Beispielen 9 und 10 ist die gleiche Stellung der Hand wie in den Beispielen 8 *a* und *b* beizubehalten. Der vorbereitete Daumen verändert nun rasch seinen Platz von F zu C und umgekehrt (siehe Bsp. 9. R. H.) ohne der Hand den geringsten Ruck zu geben; die Uebung ist *pp*, legato und staccato, auszuführen.

Beispiel 10 enthält die gleiche Bewegungsübung des Daumens, nur mit der grösseren Spannung von C zu F, welche der vollkommenen Ruhighaltung der Hand auch eine grössere Schwierigkeit entgegenstellt.

Wieder ist wie überall die schön gebogene Fingerhaltung bei hoher Stellung der Mittelhandknöchel, festen Fingerspitzen und leichtem Handgelenk, sowie horizontaler Armlage einzuhalten.

(B) Connection of Exercises Embracing only a Portion of the Scale.

The connecting of exercises 8, 9, and 10 is the foundation of a continuous scale and is to be practised as follows:

(B) Verbindung der Skalenteile.

Die Verbindung der Uebungen 8, 9 und 10 bildet die Grundlage zur fortlaufenden Skala und ist folgendermassen zu üben:

Ex. 11,
Bsp. 11.

Example 11 *a and b.* R. H.—The 2d and 3d fingers, as well as the thumb, which has been "passed under," are "prepared" on D, E, and F; the 3d strikes, holding down the key until the note struck by the thumb has sounded. At this instant the 2d and 3d fingers release their keys, and the hand and arm are shifted to the right as quickly as possible, the former keeping quite close above the keys, until the 2d, 3d, and 4th fingers are prepared on G, A, and B. The thumb accompanies this movement by slipping from one side of its key to the other. After this motion the 2d finger strikes, and is followed by the striking of the thumb, still "prepared" on F, during which latter stroke the hand and arm are again moved together, the thumb shifted along its key, until the former position has again been attained; after this the 3d finger thus "prepared" can strike again. This exercise is to be practised several times up and down, example 11 *b* being practised like 11 *a*.

NOTE.—The "preparing" of the fingers is so important that the explanation in Chapter II must be frequently referred to. The large numbers under the staff belong to the large notes and represent the playing fingers; the small numbers alongside of the small notes represent the fingers to be prepared.

(C) Preliminary Study for the Ascending Scale.

Ex. 12.

Example 12. R. H.—The thumb takes no part whatever in this example. The 2d and 3d fingers are "prepared" on D and E, and then strike simultaneously, after which the hand and arm are shifted rapidly to the right keeping close to the keys, until the 2d. 3d, and 4th fingers come to their proper position on G, A, and B, when these notes are likewise struck together. Then follows the further shifting of the hand and arm up to the position of the 2d and 3d fingers on D and

Beispiel 11 *a und b.* R. H.—Wieder stehen 2., 3. und unterlegter Daumen auf D, E und F vorbereitet; nun schlägt der 3. an und hält die Taste nieder bis zum Ertönen des anschlagenden Daumens. In demselben Augenblicke geben der 2. und 3. Finger ihre Tasten frei, und nun schiebe man die Hand raschestens und ganz nahe an den Tasten unter Begleitung des Armes nach rechts bis der 2., 3. und 4 Finger auf G, A, H vorbereitet zu stehen kommen. Der Daumen schiebt auf seiner Taste von einem Ende zum anderen mit. Hat sich nun diese Bewegung vollzogen, so schlage der 2. Finger an und bei dem darauffolgenden Anschlag des Daumens bewege sich die Hand wieder unter Begleitung des Armes und Mitschieben des Daumens auf seiner Taste in die frühere Stellung zurück und schlage der 3. an. Mehrmalige Wiederholung dieser Uebung hinauf und zurück. Beispiel 11 *b* ist wie 11 *a* zu üben.

Anmerkung.—Die Vorbereitung der Finger ist so wichtig, dass man häufig auf die Erklärung in dem zweiten Kapitel verweisen muss.

Die grossen Ziffern unter dem Linien=System gehören zu den grossen Noten und bedeuten die spielenden Finger. Die kleinen Ziffern neben den kleinen Noten bezeichnen die vorzubereitenden Finger.

(C) Vorstudie zur Fortschreitung der aufwärtsgehenden Skala.

Bsp. 12.

Beispiel 12. R. H.—Bei diesem Beispiel ist der Daumen vollkommen unbeteiligt. Der 2. und 3. Finger werden auf D, E vorbereitet und schlagen sodann gleichzeitig an. Die Hand schiebt nun unter Begleitung des Armes raschestens wieder in nächster Nähe der Tasten nach rechts, bis der 2., 3. und 4. Finger auf G, A, H vorbereitet zu stehen kommen; dieselben schlagen ebenfalls gleichzeitig an. Weiterschieben der Hand

E of the two-lined octave; so on to the conclusion of the scale, the 2d, 3d, and 4th fingers on G, A, and B. A slight turning of the elbow inward gets the hand into the straight position of Fig. 2 for the proper striking of the 5th finger when the playing of this finger is included.

This example is to be practised not only with simultaneous striking of the fingers but with them following one another.

After a thorough analysis of these exercises one may proceed to those in which the thumb takes part.

und des Armes in gleicher Weise zur Stellung des 2. und 3. auf D, E der zweigestrichenen Oktave und noch zum Schlusse der Skala 2., 3. und 4. auf G, A, H, mit geringer Drehung der Hand in die gerade Stellung von Fig. 2 für den richtigen Anschlag des 5. Fingers.

Dasselbe Beispiel ist nicht nur mit gleichzeitigem Anschlage der Finger, sondern auch mit hintereinander folgendem zu üben.

Nach Absolvierung dieser Uebungen schreite man fort zu jenen mit Beteiligung des Daumens.

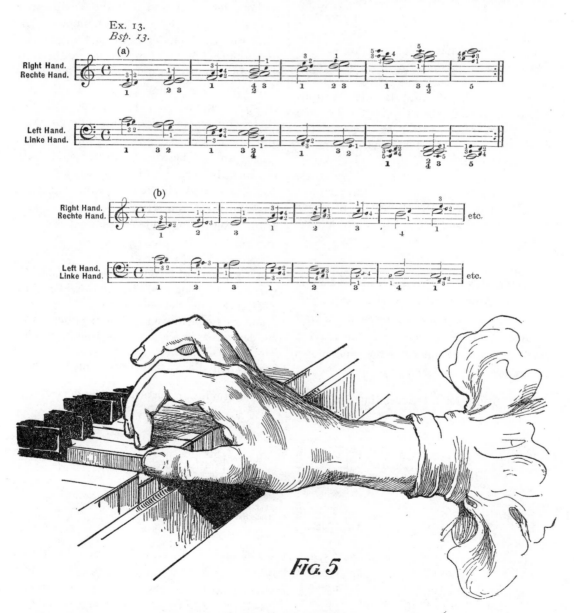

FIG. 5

Example 13 *a*. R. H.—The thumb strikes C (see Fig. 5) while the 2d and 3d fingers are "prepared" on D and E. At the moment that the two fingers strike simultaneously, the thumb "passes quickly under" on to

Beispiel 13 *a*. R. H.—Der Daumen schlägt Taste C an (siehe Fig. 5), während 2. und 3. Finger auf D und E vorbereitet stehen. Im Moment, da die beiden Finger gleichzeitig anschlagen, unterlegt sich der

F (see Fig. 6); while it strikes, the hand is again | Daumen rasch auf Taste F (siehe Fig. 6); indem er

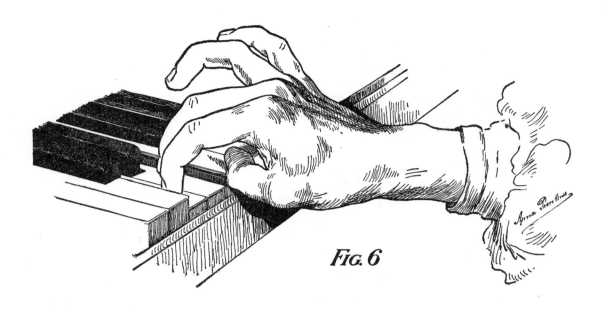

FIG. 6

shifted to the right as quickly as possible and close | anschlägt, ist die Hand wieder schnellstens und in
to the keys until the 2d, 3d, and 4th fingers are pre- | nächster Nähe der Tasten nach rechts zu schieben,
pared on G, A, and B (see Fig. 7). As these strike, | bis der 2., 3. und 4. auf G, A, H vorbereitet sind (siehe
                                           | Fig. 7). Bei ihrem Anschlag bereitet sich der Daumen

FIG. 7

the thumb is swiftly prepared on C (see Fig. 8), | schleunigst auf C vor (siehe Fig. 8), womit das Spielen

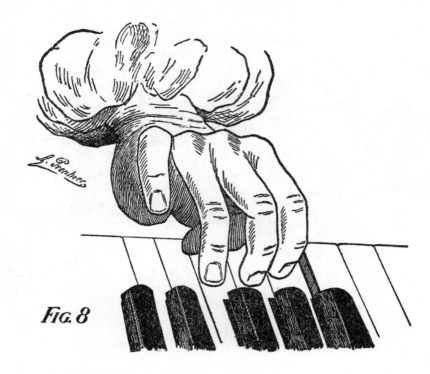

Fig. 8

and so on until the next octave is played through, and concluded with the same slight readjustment of the hand as in example 12).

After striking together the fingers are to play consecutively, leaving the keys to a raised position after striking (see Ex. 13 b, Fig. 9). This completes the

in der nächsten Oktave in eben geschilderter Weise beginnt und mit gleicher Wendung der Hand abschliesst, wie in Beispiel 12.

Auch hier wie dort werden schliesslich die Finger hintereinander gespielt, und verlassen nach ihrem Anschlag die Tasten (Bsp. 13 b, Fig. 9), was die vollendete

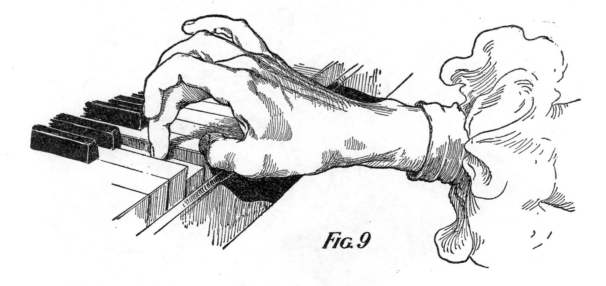

Fig. 9

ascending scale, which is now to be practised in **all keys, styles of touch** and **degrees of strength**, at first in the slowest of tempos only.

aufwärtsgehende Skala ergiebt, welche nun in allen **Tonarten, Anschlagsweisen** und **Stärkegraden,** doch vorderhand in langsamem Tempo, geübt werden soll.

II. THE DESCENDING SCALE.

(A) Passing the Fingers over the Thumb.

Position of the hand, as in figure 2, upon F, G, A, B, and C, whereupon by a slight turn of the hand inward pass the 3d and 2d fingers over on to E and D across the thumb, which remains in its original position (see Fig. 10). Examples 8, 9, and 10 (a and b)

II. ABWÄRTSGEHENDE SKALA.

(A) Das Ueberlegen der Finger.

Handstellung in Fig. 2 auf F, G, A, H, C, darauf Ueberlegen des 3. und 2. Fingers auf E, D über den liegengelassenen Daumen bei kleiner Wendung der Hand nach innen (siehe Fig. 10). Die Notenbei-

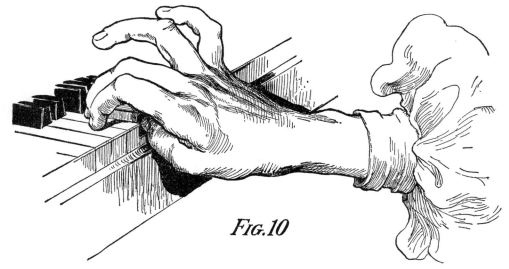

Fig. 10

of the ascending scale are now to be practised descending.

(B) Connection of Exercises Embracing only a Portion of the Scale.

Example 14 a and b.—These examples, which correspond to those of the ascending scale (Ex. 11 a and b), are to be practised in the following manner:

The hand being placed in position (Fig. 2. R. H.) on F, G, A, B, and C, the 2d finger strikes G, after which the thumb strikes F, accompanied by the simultaneous "passing over" of the 3d and 2d fingers on to E and D, accomplished by means of a slight turning of the

spiele 8, 9 und 10 (a und b) der aufwärtsgehenden Skala sind jetzt in absteigender Folge und mit dieser Handhaltung zu üben.

(B) Verbindung der Skalenteile.

Beispiel 14 a und b.—Diese Beispiele, welche mit jenen (Bsp. 11 a und b) der aufwärtsgehenden Skala korrespondieren, sind in folgender Weise zu üben:

Aus der vorbereiteten Handstellung (Fig. 2. R. H.) auf F, G, A, H, C schlägt der 2. Finger G an; darauf der Daumen F bei gleichzeitigem Ueberlegen des 3. und 2. Fingers auf E, D, unter leichter Wendung der Hand nach innen, Begleitung des Armes und Mitschieben

hand inward, the cooperation of the arm, and the sidewise shifting of the thumb. Then the 3d finger strikes, before the thumb has left its key. This is to be practised backward, the hand being brought from its inward turn back to the straight position of figure 2, as the thumb strikes and is slipped forward with the cooperation of the arm. After reaching this prepared position the 2d finger strikes, while the thumb remains motionless. This exercise should be practised several times, as also the one following, which includes the 4th finger. Care must be taken that the fingers remain as close as possible to the keys during the "passing over" motion; also that the thumb strike always *piano*.

(C) Preliminary Study for the Descending Scale.

des Daumens. Anschlag des 3. Fingers, während der Daumen seine Taste nicht verlassen hat. Dasselbe ist zurück zu üben, indem die Hand bei Anschlag und Mitschieben des Daumens unter Begleitung des Armes aus der nach innen gekehrten Lage wieder in die gerade von Fig. 2 versetzt wird. Aus dieser vorbereiteten Stellung schlägt nun der 2. bei Liegenlassen des Daumens an. Mehrmalige Wiederholung dieser Uebung und der mit Einbezug des 4. Fingers darauffolgenden. Es sei erinnert, dass die Finger bei der Bewegung des Ueberlegens in nächster Nähe der Tasten bleiben und der Daumen seinen Anschlag stets *p* ausführt.

(C) Vorstudie zur Fortschreitung der abwärtsgehenden Skala.

Ex. 15.
Bsp. 15.

Example **15.** R. H.—This example, corresponding with example **12** of the ascending scale, is, like that one practised without the thumb's taking any part. The 2d, 3d, and 4th fingers are "prepared" in a straight position on G, A, and B. The three fingers strike together, after which the hand is turned slightly inward and the 3d and 2d fingers prepared on D and E by means of a quick movement of the hand and arm. Again these two fingers strike together and the hand is moved on, in the way above described, through the next octave. This is also to be practised with the fingers' striking consecutively, the slight inward turn of the hand to be retained in both cases.

After these exercises one passes on, as in the ascending scale, to those in which the thumb takes part.

Beispiel 15. R. H.—Dieses Beispiel, mit dem Beispiel 12 der aufwärtsgehenden Skala gleichfalls korrespondierend, wird wie jenes ohne Beteiligung des Daumens geübt. Der 2., 3. und 4. Finger stehen in gerader Richtung auf G, A, H der zweigestrichenen Oktave vorbereitet. Nun gleichzeitiger Anschlag aller drei Finger, nachher kleine Wendung der Hand nach innen und mittelst raschem Ruck von Hand und Arm 3. und 2. auf E, D vorbereiten. Wieder Zusammenanschlag dieser beiden Finger und Weiterrücken in oben angegebener Weise durch die nächste Oktave hindurch. Dasselbe ist auch mit Anschlagen der Finger hintereinander zu üben und sei dabei bemerkt, dass die etwas nach innen gekehrte Handhaltung in beiden Fällen durchgängig festgehalten werden muss.

Nach diesen Uebungen gehe man, sowie bei der aufwärtsgehenden Skala, zu jenen mit Beteiligung des Daumens über.

Ex. 16.
Bsp. 16.

Example 16 *a and b*. R. H.—Hand position, figure 2, "prepared" on F, G, A, B, and C. The fifth finger strikes C, and immediately after, the 2d, 3d, and 4th, G, A, and B together. The thumb strikes F, moving from one side of its key to the other, with a quick motion of the hand and arm. The 3d and 2d fingers are simultaneously "passed over" on to D and E, prepared, and strike all together. The thumb, which has not left F, now moves under the 3d and 2d fingers on to C, is prepared upon this note, strikes, moves along the key, and then with a quick movement of the hand and arm the 2d, 3d, and 4th fingers are passed over, prepared on G, A, and B, and strike. The inward turn of the hand is constantly retained until the end is reached. Only as the thumb strikes the last C, is the position of the hand altered into the preliminary one for the ascending scale. Then follows the consecutive striking of the fingers and the playing of the descending scale entire, in which, after the thumb has struck F (of the two-lined octave, see B in Ex. 16 *a*), the slight inward turn of the hand again occurs, when the thumb leaves its key, remaining, however, underneath the hand until just before it is to strike again.

As a matter of course, everything is again to be practised in **all keys, styles of touch,** and **degrees of strength** as well as in slow time.

III. PRELIMINARY STUDIES FOR VELOCITY IN SCALE-PLAYING.

The preliminary exercises for velocity in scale-playing are taken up in this chapter because they are allied to the subject of the scale. From personal experience I recommend first the mastering in slow time of the chromatic scale, arpeggios; in fact, all the different forms, with a subsequent return to this section. The rapid playing of all exercises can then be added.

To acquire the smoothness necessary for velocity in scale-playing, one must begin by drilling the 2d and 4th fingers, which otherwise would be unequal in strength to the others. To give them the requisite

Beispiel 16 *a und b*. R. H.—Handstellung Fig. 2 auf F, G, A, H, C vorbereitet. Der 5. Finger schlägt C an, darauf der 2., 3. und 4. G, A, H gleichzeitig. Nun folgt Anschlag des Daumens auf F unter Schieben desselben an das andere Ende seiner Taste bei raschem Ruck der Hand mit Begleitung des Armes. Gleichzeitiges Ueberlegen des 3. und 2. auf E, D, Vorbereitung und Zusammenanschlag. Der Daumen, welcher F nicht verlassen hat, bewegt sich nun unter dem 3. und 2. auf C. Vorbereitung desselben bei gleichzeitigem Anschlag, Schieben auf seiner Taste, rascher Ruck der Hand und des Armes, Ueberlegen des 2., 3. und 4. Fingers, Vorbereitung auf G, A, H und Anschlag der Finger. Fortsetzung dieses Vorganges bis an das Ende der Skala. Bis zu diesem, sei noch bemerkt, muss die nach innen gekehrte Handlage beibehalten bleiben; mit dem Anschlag des Daumens auf dem letzten C verändert sie sich erst in die vorbereitende zur aufwärtsgehenden Skala. Nun erfolgt das Hintereinanderanschlagen aller Finger und das Ausspielen der abwärtsgehenden Skala, wobei nach Anschlag des Daumens auf F der zweigestrichenen Oktave wieder die leichte Wendung der Hand nach innen erfolgt und der Daumen seine Taste wohl verlässt, aber unterhalb der Hand bis zu seinem nächsten Anschlage verbleibt.

Selbstverständlich ist alles wieder in allen **Tonarten, Anschlagsweisen** und **Stärkegraden** und in langsamem Tempo zu üben.

III. VORSTUDIEN ZUM SCHNELLSPIELEN DER SKALA.

Nur um das Thema der Skala nicht zu unterbrechen, sind schon an dieser Stelle die Vorübungen für das Schnellspielen der Skala angegeben. Meinen Erfahrungen nach empfehle ich aber vor diesem Studium die nachfolgende chromatische Skala, die Arpeggien, überhaupt sämtliche Bewegungen in langsamem Tempo zu absolvieren und dann erst zu diesem Abschnitte zurückzukehren. An diesen schliesst sich auch das Schnellspielen aller Uebungen der folgenden Kapitel an.

Um bei dem Schnellspielen der Skala die vor allem richtige Gleichmässigkeit derselben zu erreichen, nehme man eine Separatbearbeitung des 2. und 4. Fingers vor, welche sonst an Kraft zurückbleiben würden.

strength, practise the following examples in this manner: Group I with particular accenting of these two fingers; Group II also with special force being exerted by the same fingers, which remain on the keys after the stroke, giving a strong, soundless second pressure; Group III with even touch of all the fingers.

Um ihnen zu dieser zu verhelfen, übe man die Beispiele in folgender Weise: Erstere (Gruppe I) mit *besonderer Betonung* der beiden Finger; die weiteren (Gruppe II) mit *besonderer Betonung* derselben und *Stehenbleiben auf den Tasten bei starkem Nachdruck;* die letzteren (Gruppe III) mit *ganz gleichem Anschlage* aller Finger.

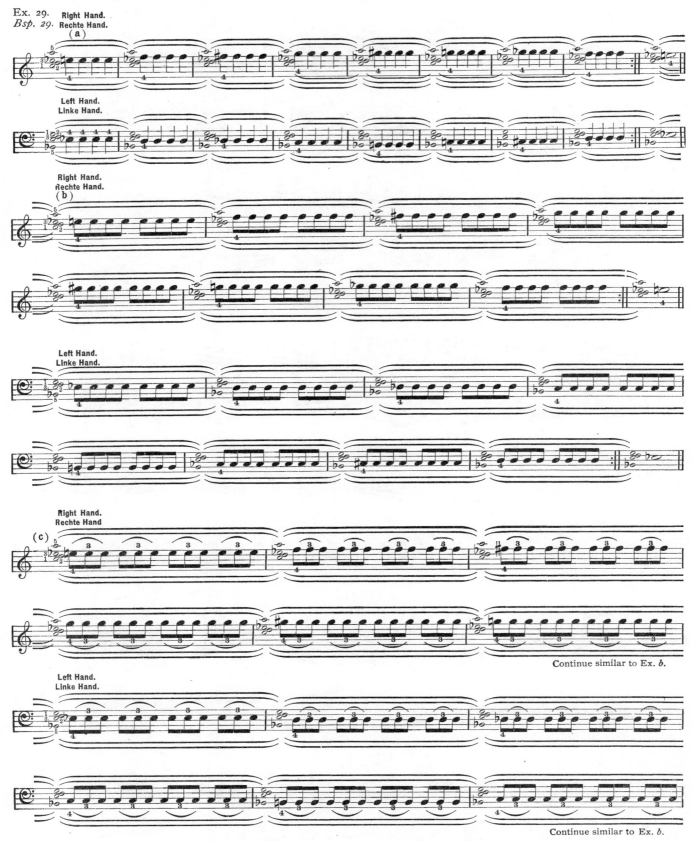

Exercises 20 to 29 are to be transposed into all keys.

Die Beispiele 20 bis 29 werden in alle Tonarten übertragen.

29

GROUP III.
GRUPPE III.

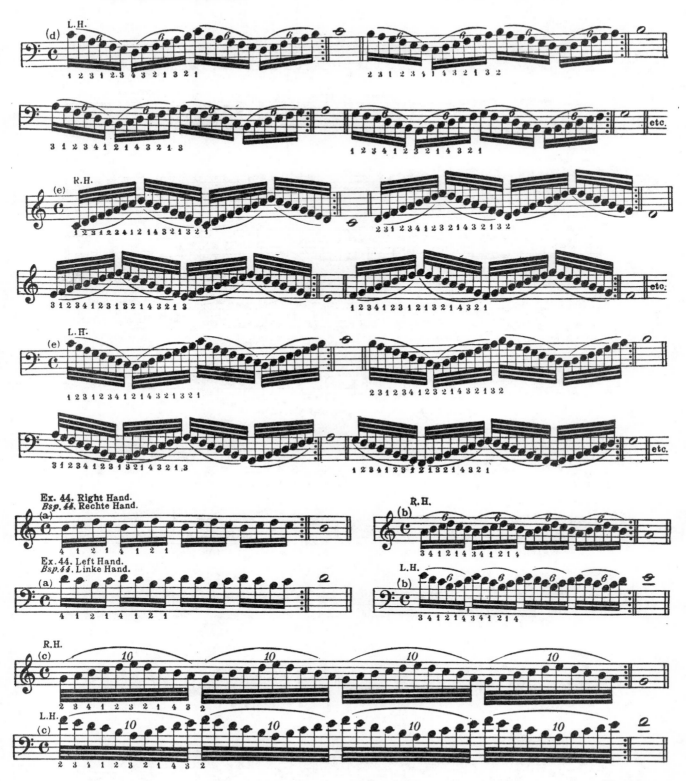

At this point the scales are to be first practised with both hands together, in octaves, thirds, sixths, tenths, and contrary motion. It is particularly helpful always to play the scale in strict rhythmic time, alternating often between groupings of six-

Die Beispiele 37 bis 44 sind in alle Tonarten zu transponieren.

Erst jetzt werden die Skalen mit beiden Händen zusammen geübt, in den wohlbekannten Oktave-, Terzen-, Dezimen-, Sextengängen und in der Gegenbewegung. Von besonderem Vorteil ist es, die Skalen

teenth and thirty-second notes, as well as thirds and sixths. In these scales, played through three or four octaves, one should keep time by counting, and not by vigorous accentuation.

As a matter of course, the same attention is to be devoted to the minor keys, all the preliminary exercises written in a major key being transposed into the minor. To alternate suddenly from playing in unison to playing in contrary motion (see Ex. 45) is very useful.

immer streng im Takt zu spielen und mit der Einteilung in Sechzehntel und Zweiunddreissigstel, sowie Triolen und Sextolen oft abzuwechseln. In diesen durch drei oder vier Oktaven gespielten Skalen halte man den Takt nur durch genaues Zählen, nicht durch hervortretende Accentuierung der einzelnen Teile ein.

Selbstverständlich widme man die gleiche Aufmerksamkeit den Molltonarten und übertrage alle in Dur geschriebenen Vorübungen nach Moll.

Von grossem Nutzen ist auch die plötzliche Abwechslung des Unisonospieles mit der Gegenbewegung, z. B.:

Ex. 45.
Bsp. 45.

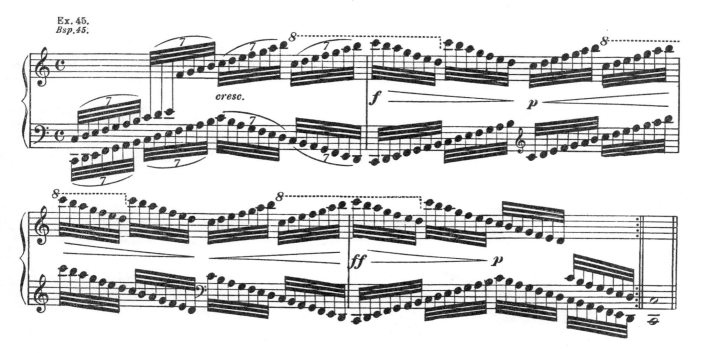

The various styles of touch and degrees of strength must be practised in quick time also.

In scale-playing the fingers are as curved on the black keys as on the white. This is different in chord-stretches, arpeggios, and "cantilene" playing, where the fingers must be decidedly flatter when striking the black keys to further ensure safety against slipping.

Natürlich wende man auch im schnellen Tempo verschiedene Anschlagsarten und Stärkegrade an.

Noch sei erwähnt, dass in Skalen mit Obertasten die Haltung der Finger auf letzteren eine ebenso gebogene sei, als auf weissen Tasten; anders ist es in Accordgriffen, Arpeggien und in der Kantilene, wo die Finger auf schwarzen Tasten bedeutend flacher anschlagen müssen.

CHAPTER IV.

THE CHROMATIC SCALE.

ASCENDING SCALE

KAPITEL IV.

DIE CHROMATISCHE SKALA.

AUFWÄRTSGEHENDE SKALA.

Ex. 46.
Bsp. 46.

Right Hand.

The position of the hand and arm is the same for the chromatic as for the diatonic scale: the wrist slightly raised; the knuckles held particularly high. The following exercises are to be practised legato; **the thumb always** *pp*.

Rechte Hand.

Die Hand- und Armhaltung bei der chromatischen Skala gleicht jener der diatonischen: Handgelenk etwas erhöht, die Mittelhandknöchel besonders hoch. Sämtliche Uebungen sind legato auszuführen **Daumen stets** *pp*.

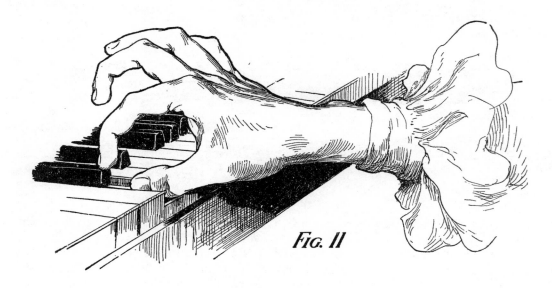

FIG. II

Ex. 47.
Bsp. 47.
(a)

(b)

(c)

Example 47 *a.*—In this example the thumb is prepared on C, the 2d finger on D flat (the "enharmonic" change from C sharp to D flat is made for the sake of plainness in writing). At first the fingers move slowly while one counts up to 4. As shown in Fig. 11, the thumb strikes the center of the white key with its extreme point, while the 2d, curved, plays on the very edge of the black key.

In this exercise as well as in those following, the thumb strikes universally *p*. In Ex. 47 *c* the fingers practise, trill fashion, in very slow time.

In Ex. 48 the thumb is again prepared on C and the 2d finger on C sharp. The thumb strikes, then the 2d finger, whereupon the thumb quickly leaves its key, prepares on D and strikes. After this the 2d finger strikes, the thumb meanwhile returning to C. This thumb exercise is to be repeated several times.

Example 49.—The 2d finger is prepared on C sharp, the thumb on D. The 2d finger strikes, followed by the striking of the thumb; as this finger is shifted forward on its key with a corresponding movement of the arm, the 2d finger is quickly prepared on D sharp, and strikes.

While the thumb strikes and is shifted backward the 2d finger is again quickly prepared on C sharp, and strikes. This exercise is to be practised up and down, several times.

Beispiel 47 *a.*—In diesen Beispielen werden der Daumen auf C, der 2. auf *Des* (der klaren Schreibweise wegen enharmonische Verwechslung von Cis in Des) gemeinsam vorbereitet. Zuerst werden die Finger einzeln unter langsamem Zählen von 1 bis 4 geübt. Wie in Fig. 11 ersichtlich, schlägt der Daumen auf seiner äussersten Spitze in der Mitte der weissen Taste an, der 2. sehr gebogen am äussersten Rande der schwarzen Taste.

In diesen, wie allen folgenden Uebungen, ist der Daumen *p* anzuschlagen. In Beispiel 47 *c* üben die Finger in trillerartiger Weise in langsamstem Tempo.

In Beispiel 48 wieder Vorbereitung des Daumens auf C und des 2. auf Des. Daumen schlägt an, dann 2. Finger, wobei der Daumen seine Taste rasch verlässt, um sich unter dem 2. auf D vorzubereiten und anzuschlagen. Nun Anschlag des 2., wobei der Daumen wieder auf C zurückkehrt. Mehrmalige Wiederholung dieser Daumenübung.

Beispiel 49.—Vorbereitung des 2. auf Cis und des Daumens auf D. Anschlag des 2., darauffolgender Anschlag des Daumens, während seines Schiebens an das andere Ende der Taste unter begleitender Bewegung des Armes, rasche Vorbereitung des 2. Fingers auf Dis und Anschlag desselben.

Während Anschlag des Daumens und Zurückschieben desselben, wieder rasche Vorbereitung des 2. Fingers auf Cis mit darauffolgendem Anschlag. Mehrmals hin und her zu üben.

Ex. 50.
Bsp. 50.
(a)

Example 50.—(The "enharmonic" change, F sharp to G flat, has been made for the sake of clearness in writing.) In Ex. 50 *a*, *b*, and *c*, the thumb, 2d and 3d fingers are prepared on E, F, and G flat; at first each finger is practised separately, then the thumb and 2d finger, and 2d and 3d alternately. After this, all three fingers play consecutively up and down, the thumb always *p*.

Beispiel 50.—(Der klaren Schreibweise wegen wurde in Beispiel 50 mit dem Fis der aufwärtsgehenden Skala die enharmonische Verwandlung in Ges vorgenommen.) In Beispiel 50 *a*, *b*, *c*, stehen Daumen, 2. und 3. Finger auf E, F, Ges vorbereitet. Zuerst Ueben der einzelnen Finger; dann Daumen und 2., 2. und 3. Finger mit einander abwechselnd; darauf Hintereinanderspielen aller drei Finger auf und ab; wie schon erwähnt, Daumen stets *p*.

Example 51.—This thumb exercise must be practised exactly as in the diatonic scale, *piano*, legato, and staccato, the only difference being that the thumb, when it has passed under, does not strike on the edge of the key but in the center; as is the rule throughout the chromatic scale.

Beispiel 51.—Diese Daumenübung ist wie jene der diatonischen Tonleiter zu üben und auch *p*, legato und staccato, auszuführen. Als einziger Unterschied greift der Daumen bei dem Untersetzen nicht an den Rand, sondern in die Mitte der Taste, wie überhaupt bei seinem Anschlag in der ganzen chromatischen Skala.

Ex. 52 includes the 3d finger in the ascending chromatic scale.

Beispiel 52 zeigt noch das Mitspielen des 3. Fingers in der aufwärtsgehenden chromatischen Skala.

THE DESCENDING CHROMATIC SCALE.

ABWÄRTSGEHENDE CHROMATISCHE SKALA.

Ex. 53.
Bsp. 53.

Fingering: 3 1 3 1 3 1 3 2 1 3 1 3 1
Fingersatz:

Right Hand.

Example 53.—The descending chromatic scale must also be given attention in detail, and as in the descending diatonic scale the hand is turned slightly inward.

Rechte Hand.

Beispiel 53.—Auch die abwärtsgehende chromatische Skala ist bei dem Vorstudium in kleine Teile zu zerlegen und wird, gleichwie in der diatonischen abwärtsgehenden Skala, die etwas nach innen gekehrte Handhaltung angewendet.

The ascending and descending chromatic scale **must** be first practised in slow time, various styles of touch and degrees of strength.

Same exercises for left hand.

Die auf- und abwärtsgehende chromatische Skala ist vorerst in langsamem Tempo, in verschiedenen Anschlagsarten und Stärkegraden, zu üben.

Uebertragung auf die linke Hand.

For the sake of greater clearness in writing, the enharmonic changes are made here also.

All the rules given for the right hand, ascending scale, are applicable to the left, descending scale, and *vice versâ*.

Like the diatonic scale, the chromatic scale must be practised with both hands in octaves, thirds, tenths, sixths, and contrary motion as well as in unison and contrary motion mixed, in all degrees of strength, rapidity and variations of time.

Der klareren Schreibweise wegen, wird zuweilen B in Ais, As in Gis auf enharmonische Weise verwandelt.

Selbstverständlich ist alles für die aufwärtsgehende Skala der rechten Hand Gesagte für die abwärtsgehende der linken Hand giltig, und umgekehrt.

Gleich dem Muster der diatonischen Tonleiter ist auch die chromatische mit beiden Händen in Oktaven, Terzen, Dezimen, Sexten und Gegenbewegung, sowie der Mischung von Unisono- und Gegenbewegung, in allen Stärke- und Schnelligkeitsgraden mit verschiedenster Takteinteilung zu üben.

CHAPTER V.	KAPITEL V.
THE TRILL.	TRILLER.

Example 54 a. — Position of the hand and fingers that of Fig. 2. The unemployed fingers must be held perfectly still while the trill is practised, and may either press the keys down or simply lie "prepared" upon them; the latter way is the more difficult. The trill is practised legato, crescendo, and with an increase of tempo from slow to fast and very fast.

After this, practise changing the fingers on the same trill; by this means one can trill a long while without wearying the fingers. The change must be made so adroitly that the introduction of the new finger is not audible (see Ex. 55).

Beispiel 54 a.—Hand- und Fingerstellung von Fig. 2. Während der Trillerübungen regungslose Haltung der unbeschäftigten Finger, welche entweder die Tasten niederdrücken oder auf denselben blos vorbereitet stehen, was noch schwerer ist. Die trillernden Finger spielen legato, *p* beginnend bis zum *f*, aus dem langsamen Tempo die Schnelligkeit nach und nach entwickelnd.

Dann übe man das Abwechseln der Finger auf gleichen Tasten, wodurch man eine grosse Ausdauer im Trillern entfalten kann, was aber mit solcher Geschicklichkeit geschehen muss, dass man den Einsatz des neuen Fingers nicht hört (siehe Bsp. 55).

The strongest fingers are used for a *forte* trill; for instance, the 3d and thumb or 3d and 5th (see Lit. Ex. 1).

Bei Fortetrillern kommen die stärksten Finger in Anwendung; z. B. 3. und Daumen oder 3. und 5. (siehe Lit. Bsp. 1).

BEETHOVEN, Op. 73.

The use of the 3d finger and thumb is recommended when possible, for greater clearness,—Liszt's Rhapsodie No. 8 (see Lit. Ex. 2).

3. Finger und Daumen anzuwenden, ist auch in vielen Fällen blos der Klarheit wegen sehr günstig; z. B. Liszt: aus Rhapsodie Nr. 8 (siehe Lit. Bsp 2).

LISZT, RHAPSODIE, No. 8.

In a *forte* trill "al" decrescendo, one commences with the strongest fingers changing to those which from their nature would produce a weaker sound (see Illustration I, bar 4).

In modern music, for the sake of greater effect, the trill can be delivered with the utmost possible strength by making use of both hands; in this case, to make the transition smoother, the conclusion of the trill is usually played by one hand only.

It is advisable to begin a trill with a well-nigh simultaneous striking of the first two notes coupled with a slight impulse from the wrist (see Illustration III). To start the trill with extreme brilliancy, one

Bei einem Fortetriller, weicher decrescendiert werden soll, wende man an der Fortestelle die oben erwähnten stärksten Finger an und gehe dann in die in dieser Lage schwächer klingenden über (siehe Literatur-Beispiel I, Takt 4).

Um in modernen Stücken einen besonderen Effekt zu erzielen, kann der Triller in höchst möglichem Stärkegrad mit Beteiligung beider Hände gemacht werden, wobei der Schluss des Trillers, des Ueberganges wegen, gewöhnlich von *einer* Hand ausgeführt wird.

Sehr günstig ist es, den Triller mit leichtem Wurf des Handgelenkes und beinahe zusammenanschlagenden Fingern zu beginnen (siehe Literatur-Beispiel III).

SAINT-SAENS, Op. 22.

hand can strike the principal note while the other, beginning with the alternate note, continues the trill. This makes the playing of a series of trills particularly easy; the trill coming at the climax can then be played with both hands (see Illustration IV).

Um den Einsatz des Trillers besonders zu markieren, kann eine Hand die Hauptnote anschlagen, während die andere, mit der Wechselnote beginnend, den Triller fortsetzt. Diese Spielweise bietet eine besondere Erleichterung für Trillerketten; der höchste und stärkste Triller kann dann mit beiden Händen ausgeführt werden (siehe Literatur-Beispiel IV).

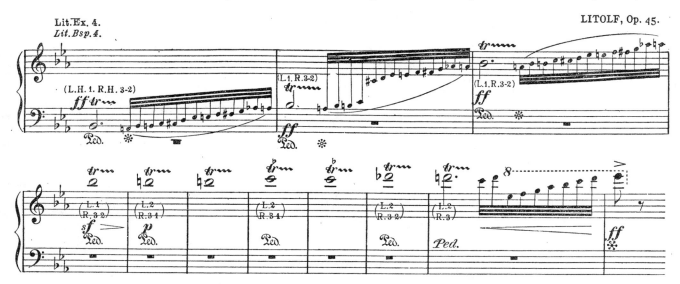

LITOLF, Op. 45.

In a chain of trills played with one hand (see Illustration V) or in any succession of trills where a melody is carried out (see Illustration VI), the principal note or notes of the melody must be struck with special emphasis, without, however, disturbing the smoothness of the trill.

Bei der mit nur einer Hand ausgeführten Trillerkette (siehe Literatur-Beispiel V), oder einer Reihe von Trillern, welche eine melodiöse Bedeutung haben (siehe Literatur-Beispiel VI), müssen die Haupt-oder Melodienoten besonders klar angeschlagen werden ohne den Fluss des Trillers zu stören.

BEETHOVEN, Op. 73

Lit. Ex 5
Lit Bsp 5

BEETHOVEN, Op. 73.

Lit. Ex 6.
Lit. Bsp. 6

Where the left hand is disengaged (see Illustration VII) a trill can be played in many different ways. One of the ways by which such a trill may be facilitated is given below:

Literatur-Beispiel VII lässt sich durch das Freiwerden der linken Hand auf die verschiedenste Art und Weise ausführen. Eine dieser Versionen, die alle dem Zwecke der Erleichterung dienen, sei hier angegeben:

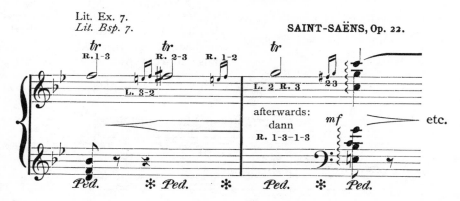

Lit. Ex. 7.
Lit. Bsp. 7.

SAINT-SAËNS, Op. 22.

Most difficult of all are those trill passages—as, for example, Beethoven: Op. 111, end of the last movement (see Illustration. VIII)—where neither the melody nor the trill can be interrupted.

Am schwierigsten sind Trillerstellen, wie z. B Beethoven Op. 111, Ende des letzten Satzes (siehe Literatur-Beispiel VIII), wo weder das Thema noch der Triller unterbrochen werden darf.

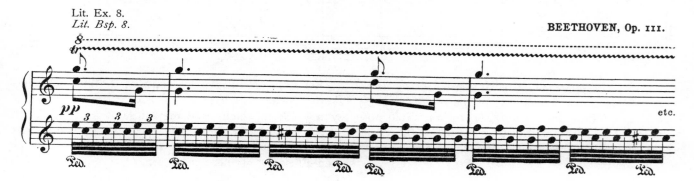

Lit. Ex. 8.
Lit. Bsp. 8.

BEETHOVEN, Op. 111.

CHAPTER VI.
THE CHORD.
TRIAD. CHORD OF THE SEVENTH.

Chord practice is one of the best forms of exercise for stretching the hand. Place the hand on any chord, as, for example, on the triad of C major.

KAPITEL VI.
DER ACCORD.
DREIKLANG. SEPTACCORD.

Die Aufstellung und Uebung der Finger in Accordform ist eine der ausgezeichnetsten Dehnübungen für die Hand. Man stelle dieselbe in irgend einem Accord, z. B. Dreiklang C Dur auf:

Fig. 12

Right Hand.

The extreme point of the thumb is on the edge of key C, the 2d finger in the middle of key E, the 3d near the black keys on G (both fingers well curved), the 5th somewhat extended on the edge of C. The position of the hand shows a slight turn outward. In order to keep the fingers well separated, the keys lying between them may be pulled up above the surface of the keyboard (see Chap. 1). The fingers are first practised separately and then legato consecutively (see Ex. 56):

Rechte Hand.

Daumen mit der äussersten Spitze am Rande der Taste C, 2. Finger in der Mitte der Taste E, 3. nahe den schwarzen Tasten auf G (beide Finger schön gebogen), 5. etwas gestreckt am Rande der Taste C. Die Lage der Hand zeigt eine leichte Wendung nach auswärts. Um den Fingern eine gute Stütze zu geben, kann man die zwischen denselben liegenden Tasten über die Fläche der Klaviatur heraufziehen (siehe Kap. 1). Zuerst übe man jeden Finger einzeln, dann die Verbindung der Finger untereinander (siehe Bsp. 56).

Ex. 56.
Bsp. 56.

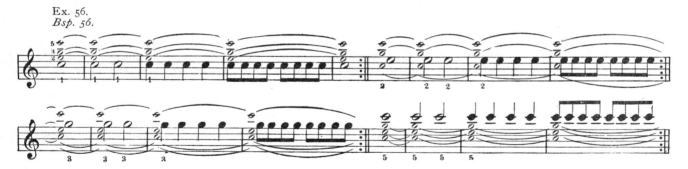

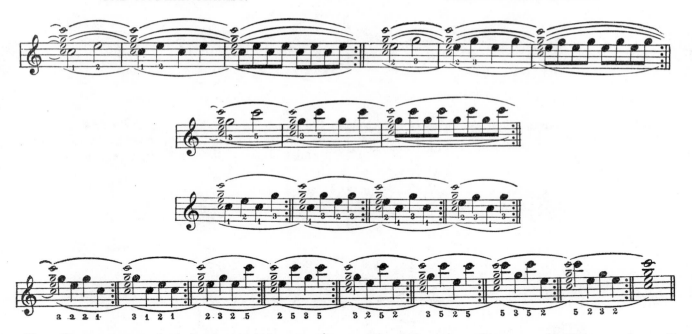

The still greater stretch of the chord of the seventh, for instance the dominant seventh chord of C major with octave, is developed by the following exercises, which correspond with those of the triad: Ex. 57.

Die noch grössere Spannung des Septaccordes, z. B Dominantseptaccord von C Dur mit der Oktave, wird durch folgende Uebungen ausgebildet, welche mit jenen des Dreiklanges correspondieren: Bsp. 57).

Ex. 57.
Bsp. 57.

Ex. 58.
Bsp. 58.

Ex. 59.
Bsp. 59.

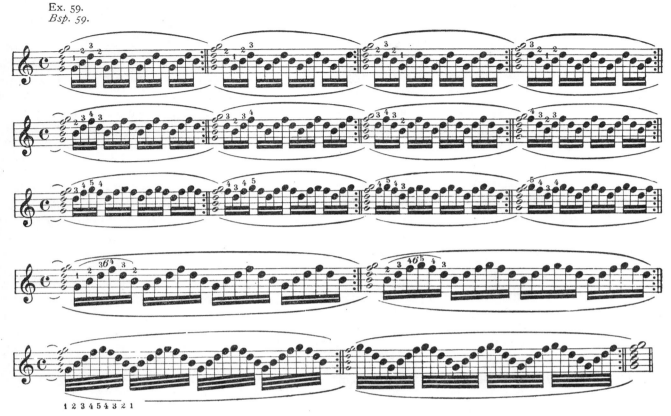

A strong, firm touch is to be used with all these exercises, the keys being held down after the stroke; the arm and wrist position as already given. With the fingers in position and their hold on the keys unrelaxed, the wrist is again to be raised and lowered according to the model in Chapter I, Fig. 3.

After this exercise follows the study of the striking of the chords from the wrist (see Fig. 13). Care being

Sämtliche Beispiele sind mit kräftigem Anschlage unter nachherigem Liegenlassen der Finger nach den bisher gegebenen Regeln der Arm- und Handgelenkshaltung auszuführen. Bei unveränderter Fingerhaltung in Accordform unter festem Niederdrücken der Tasten ist auch das Handgelenk nach Muster des Kapitels I, Fig. 3 zu üben.

An diese Uebungen schliesst sich das Studium des Accordgriffes aus dem Handgelnke an (siehe Fig. 13).

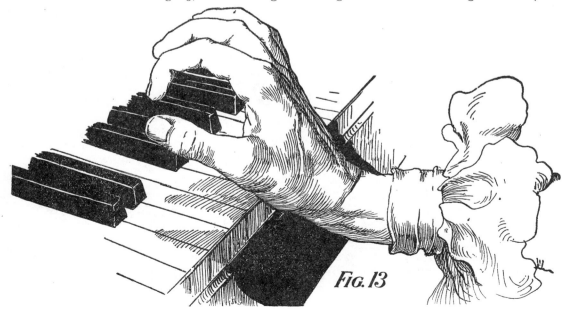

FIG. 13

taken to place the hand in correct position, it is raised from the wrist and then bent back as far as possible, while one counts very slowly from 1 to 4, the fingers keeping unchanged the shape required by the chord. It then falls quickly back on the place just deserted, remaining there for a longer or shorter time, the latter alternative being the more difficult. By means of this exercise one acquires certainty in striking the chords. In chords the fingers are placed somewhat flatter upon the black keys than in scale-playing. In contrast to the general outward turn of the hand some chords, rarely encountered, demand a slight turn of the hand inward. It is well to practise the chords first *p*, and then *f*. In order to increase one's certainty, practise chord playing from the wrist to and fro from one octave into another.

After this section follows the co-operation of the arm, in order to develop strength in manipulating chords. Sonorous chords are executed in the following different ways: The fingers are placed in readiness on the keys, which they strike strongly with the full assistance of the arm, whereupon the wrist by a slight depression and then a return to its normal height, relaxes the strain of the arm, thus avoiding any fatigue during the holding down of the chord.

Short-sounding chords should be practised in two different ways. Either the fingers take the form necessitated by the chord while raised, falling in that shape from above on to the keys, striking them quickly and leaving them as quickly with a slight throwing of the wrist upward; or the fingers are first prepared on the keys before playing. After striking in the latter way the wrist may be either depressed or swung upward; it is good to practise both ways, as thereby strength and elasticity are attained at the same time.

The following group of chords (Ex. 62), not written with any idea of harmonic progression, lends itself best to the foregoing practise through multiplicity and variety in chord "stretches."

Man stelle die Hand in einem Accorde präcis auf, hebe sie dann unter langsamem Zählen von 1 bis 4 nur aus dem Gelenke empor, biege sie so weit als möglich zurück, wobei die Finger das Accordbild unverändert festhalten, und falle dann rasch wieder auf den verlassenen Platz herab mit längerem oder auch ganz kurzem Verweilen darauf, welch' letzteres Vorgehen der kaum unterbrochenen Wiederholung wegen schwieriger, aber sehr nützlich ist. Der Zweck dieser Uebung ist die Treffsicherheit der Accordgriffe. Bei Accorden mit Obertasten sind die Finger ungleich der Skala mit Obertasten, etwas flacher auf dieselben aufzustellen, und manche Accordphysiognomie erfordert im Gegensatz zu der zumeist nach aussen gekehrten Handwendung eine leichte Neigung der Handhaltung nach innen, was aber selten vorkommt. Es ist gut, die Accorde erst *p*, dann *f* zu üben.

Um die Treffsicherheit noch zu erhöhen, übe man den Accordwurf aus dem Handgelenk von einer Oktave in die andere hin und her. Nach diesem Abschnitte tritt zur Ausbildung der Kraft im Accordgriffe die Mitwirkung des Armes hinzu. Getragene Accorde werden folgendermassen ausgeführt: Die Finger stehen vorbereitet auf den Tasten, welche sie mit voller Unterstützung des Armes kräftig anschlagen, worauf aber das Handgelenk durch eine leichte Senkung und Zurückhebung in die normale Höhe die Spannung des Armes aufhebt und dadurch jeder Ermüdung bei dem Weiterhalten des Accordes vorbeugt.

Kurzklingende Accorde sind auf zweierlei Arten zu üben; entweder fallen die Finger mit vorbereitetem Accordbild aus der Höhe auf die Tastatur, den Accord sofort anschlagend und die Tasten ebenso rasch mit leichtem Wurf des Handgelenkes nach aufwärts wieder verlassend, oder die Finger befinden sich in Vorbereitung auf den Tasten vor Anschlag der Accorde. Nach Anschlag der letzteren kann das Handgelenk schnell nach abwärts geschleudert oder in die Höhe geschwungen werden; es ist gut, beides zu üben, da man dabei Kraft und zugleich Elasticität erzielt.

Alle Spielweisen werden am besten in folgender Accordgruppe ausgeführt, welche nicht eine durch die Gesetze der Harmonielehre bedingte Reihenfolge in sich schliesst, sondern nur dem Zweck der Mannigfaltigkeit und Abwechslung der Accordgriffe entspricht:

Ex. 62.
Bsp. 62.

These chords are also to be played broken, care being taken that the sounds follow each other in as close a succession as possible. For this the preparing of the fingers is all important; a rapid turn of the hand in the direction of the little finger or the thumb, according as the broken chords are played upward or downward (see Ex. 63 *a* and *b*), will help to make the notes sound almost simultaneously (see Ex. 63).

Auch auf arpeggierte Weise spiele man diese Gruppe, indem man bei den Arpeggien bedacht sei, die Töne möglichst nahe an einander gereiht erklingen zu lassen, was durch Vorbereitung der Finger in Accordform und darauf erfolgendem Anschlag, beinahe Zusammenanschlag der Finger unter raschester Wendung der Hand in die Richtung des 5. oder umgekehrt des Daumens geschieht, je nachdem sie auf- oder abwärts arpeggiert werden sollen (siehe Bsp. 63).

This group of chords is to be transposed into all the different keys. Exercises of great value for the flexibility of the fingers can be made out of them (see Ex. 64 *a*).

Die Accordgruppe ist in alle Tonarten zu transponieren. Für die Beweglichkeit der Finger sind die aus dieser Gruppe sich bildenden Uebungen von grossem Nutzen (siehe Bsp. 64 *a*).

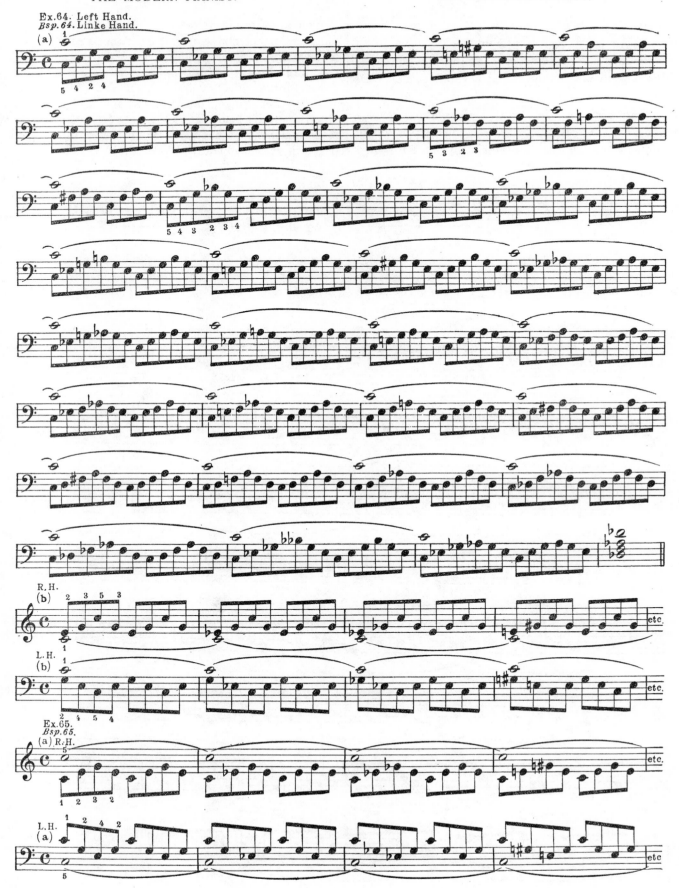

All examples are to be carried out according to the form of exercise 64 *a*, and are to be transposed into all keys.

Alle Beispiele sind nach dem Musterbeispiel 64 *a* auszuführen und in sämtliche Tonarten zu transponieren.

CHAPTER VII

ARPEGGIOS.

I. THE ASCENDING ARPEGGIO.

Right Hand.

The study of the arpeggio follows that of the chord. It is important that the exercises in this chapter be practised legato, since that constitutes their greatest difficulty.

(A) Passing the Thumb under the Hand.

TRIAD OF C MAJOR.

As in the scale, passing the thumb under the hand constitutes the main difficulty in arpeggio playing. As assistance the following exercises are given:

KAPITEL VII.

ARPEGGIEN.

I. AUFWÄRTSGEHENDE ARPEGGIEN.

Rechte Hand.

Dem Studium des Accordes folgt das Studium der Arpeggien. Hier sei besonders betont, dass die diesbezüglichen Uebungen legato ausgeführt werden sollen, da sie in dieser Anschlagsart am schwierigsten sind.

(A) Das Untersetzen des Daumens.

DREIKLANG C DUR.

Wie bei der Skala ist auch hier das Untersetzen des Daumens eine Hauptschwierigkeit und mache man daher folgende Uebungen:

Example 71.—The 3d finger and the thumb (see Fig. 14) stand, as in commencing the scale, somewhat

Der 3. Finger und der Daumen (siehe Fig. 14 u. Bsp 71) stehen wie im Beginn der Skala in etwas schiefer

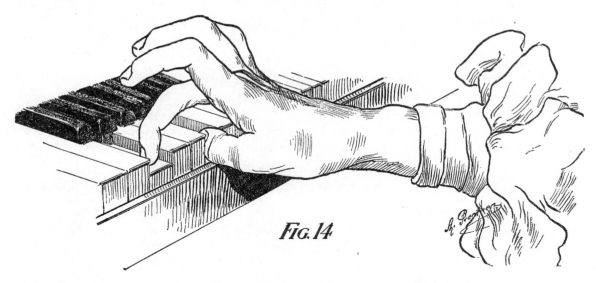

FIG. 14

at an angle to the keys. The thumb, passed under on to C, strikes the note softly with its extreme point, and rises with the note during the slow counting of 1 to 4. Repeat several times, then practice in the same way with the 3d finger. After this, the thumb and 3d finger play alternately, the former *p*, the latter *f*.

Richtung zu den Tasten. Der auf C unterlegte Daumen schlage mit seiner äussersten Spitze schwach an, erhebe sich mit der Taste unter langsamem Zählen von 1 bis 4 und wiederhole dies mehrere Male; ganz gleich übt der 3. Darauf abwechselnd Daumen und 3.; ersterer *p*, letzterer laut.

(B) Connecting the Arpeggio Parts.

The following exercise forms the foundation of arpeggio playing:

(B) Verbindung der Arpeggienteile.

Folgende Uebung bildet die Grundlage zu dem Ausspielen der Arpeggien:

Ex. 72.
Bsp. 72.

Example 72.—The 3d finger and the thumb "passed under," are prepared on G and C; the 3d finger strikes and remains upon its key until the thumb strikes C; simultaneously with this the 3d finger releases G, and with a rapid turn of the hand to the right, accompanied by a forward movement of the arm and the shifting of the thumb upon its key, the 2d and 3d fingers are "prepared" upon the keys E and G. The fingers in passing over keep as close to the keys as possible. After finishing this movement the 2d finger strikes E, the thumb following with C, while the hand moves backward to its former position, the 3d finger striking G. This exercise should be repeated several times.

Wieder sind 3. Finger und unterlegter Daumen auf den Tasten G und C vorbereitet; der 3. schlägt an und wartet auf seiner Taste bis der Daumen C anschlägt. Im gleichen Momente verlässt der 3. G, wobei die Hand mit raschem Ruck nach rechts unter Mitschieben des Armes und des Daumens auf seiner Taste den 2. und 3. über den Daumen hinweg auf E, G vorbereitet. Das Ueberlegen ist wieder in nächster Nähe der Tasten auszuführen. Nach Vollziehung dieser Bewegung, Anschlag des 2. Fingers auf E, darauf des Daumens auf C, wobei sich die Hand in oben beschriebener Weise zurückbewegt. In dieser ersten Lage Anschlag des 3 auf G Wiederholung dieser Uebung mehrere Male

(C) The Ascending Arpeggio.

It is useful to extend the arpeggio practice through three octaves.

(C) Ausspielen der aufwärtsgehenden Arpeggien.

Es ist zweckmässig, die Arpeggien etwas ausgedehnter als die Skalen zu üben, nämlich durch drei Oktaven hindurch.

Example 73.—Prepare the fingers on C, E, and G. The thumb strikes C (Fig. 15). As the 2d finger

Beispiel 73.—Vorbereitung der Finger auf C, E, G. Anschlag des Daumens auf C (siehe Fig. 15); bei nun

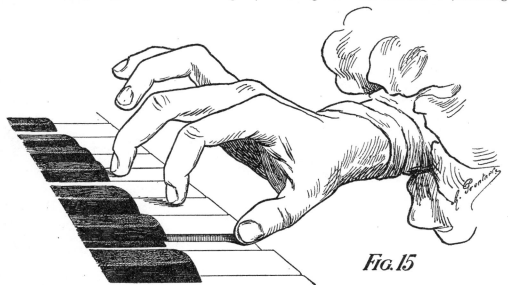

Fig. 15

strikes E, the thumb disappears quickly under the hand in the direction of the octave C (Fig. 16). The

erfolgendem Anschlag des 2., rasches Verschwinden des Daumens unter die Hand in die Richtung des oberen C (Fig. 16). Anschlag des 3., wobei der 2. sich von der

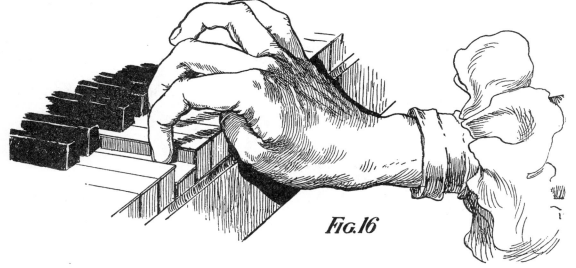

Fig. 16

3d finger strikes, while the 2d is lifted from its key and the thumb prepared on C (see Fig. 17). As this

Taste erhebt und sich der Daumen direkt auf C vorbereitet (Fig. 17). Bei Anschlag desselben und

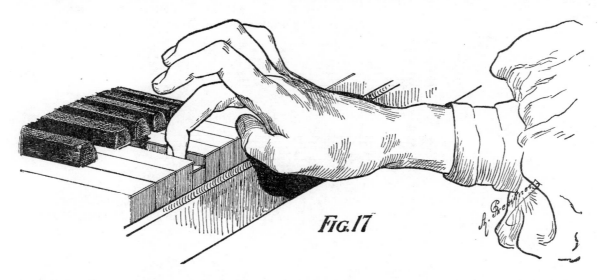

FIG. 17

strikes and is shifted forward on its key, the 2d and 3d fingers are rapidly passed over, keeping close to the keys and prepared on E and G. This is to be repeated through the next octave; the last octave to be played with the fingers, prepared as for a chord, keeping in contact with their keys until the 2d and 3d fingers are passed back over the thumb in descending. This is to be practised in slow time, in all keys, styles of touch, and gradations of strength. Here, too, the thumb always strikes piano.

Schieben auf seiner Taste unter Begleitung des Armes, rasches Ueberlegen des 2. und 3. Fingers ganz nahe den Tasten E, G. Weiterspielen wie früher; letzte Oktave mit Vorbereitung des Accordes ausspielen und die Finger nicht mehr aufheben. Gleich der Skala in allen Tonarten, Anschlagsweisen und Stärkegraden in langsamem Tempo zu üben. Der Daumen schlägt auch hier stets *p* an.

II. THE DESCENDING ARPEGGIOS.

(A) Passing the Fingers over the Thumb.

Right Hand.

Position of the hand as in Fig. 12. The 3d and 2d fingers are passed over the thumb with a slight turn of the hand inward, and prepared on to G and E respectively, the thumb being left in position on its key. (Proceed as in the descending scale.) The examples given in No. 71 of the ascending arpeggio are to be practised descending with the hand turned slightly inward.

(B) Connecting the Arpeggio Parts.

II. ABWÄRTSGEHENDE ARPEGGIEN.

(A) Das Ueberlegen der Finger.

Rechte Hand.

Handstellung in Fig. 12; darauf Ueberlegen des 3. und 2. Fingers auf G, E, über den liegengelassenen Daumen bei kleiner Wendung der Hand nach innen. (Vorgehen wie in der abwärtsgehenden Skala.) Die Notenbeispiele Nr. 71 der aufwärtsgehenden Arpeggien sind in absteigender Folge mit nach innen gekehrter Handhaltung zu üben.

(B) Verbindung der Arpeggienteile.

Example 74.—The hand in the position of Fig. 12, triad of C major, the 2d finger strikes E and is followed immediately by the thumb's striking C. Simultaneously with this the 3d and 2d fingers are quickly passed over and prepared on G and E, the hand together with the wrist being turned slightly inward. The 3d finger then strikes, while the thumb still remains on its key. This is to be practised backward the hand resuming its straightened position (Fig. 12) on its return. Proceeding down the C major triad the thumb strikes and moves forward with the wrist, the 2d and 3d fingers being again quickly prepared on G and C. This is to be repeated several times, the 2d and 3d fingers *f*, the thumb *p*.

Beispiel 74.—Aus der vorbereiteten Handstellung Fig. 12, Dreiklang C Dur, schlägt der 2. E an; darauf der Daumen C bei gleichzeitigem Ueberlegen des 3. und 2. Fingers auf G und E unter leichter Wendung der Hand nach innen und Drehung des Handgelenkes. Anschlag des 3. Fingers, während der Daumen seine Taste nicht verlassen hat. Dasselbe ist zurück zu üben, indem die Hand bei Anschlag und Mitschieben des Daumens unter Begleitung des Handgelenkes aus der nach innen gekehrten Lage wieder in die erste gerade Stellung Fig. 12, Dreiklang C Dur, versetzt wird. Aus dieser vorbereiteten Stellung schlägt nun der 2. bei Liegenlassen des Daumens an. Mehrmalige Wiederholung dieser Uebung; 2. und 3. laut, Daumen *p*.

(C) The Descending Arpeggio.   (C) Ausspielen der abwärtsgehenden Arpeggien.

Ex. 75.
Bsp. 75.

Right Hand.

Example 75.—Position of hand as in Fig. 12.

Triad of C major prepared. The 5th finger strikes C, the 3d and the 2d following in their turn. The thumb strikes C, at the same time shifting to the other side of its key with a quick turn of the hand inward from the wrist (Fig. 18). The 3d and 2d fingers are

Rechte Hand.

Beispiel 75.—Handstellung Fig. 12.

Dreiklang C Dur vorbereitet. Der 5. Finger schlägt C an, darauf der 3. und 2. der Reihe nach. Nun Anschlag des Daumens auf C unter Rückung an das andere Ende der Taste bei rascher Wendung der Hand nach innen aus dem Handgelenke (Fig. 18). Ueberlegen des

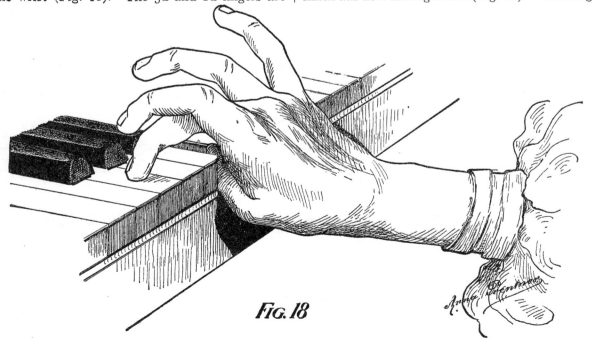

FIG. 18

"passed over," and the 3d prepared on G, which is struck. The thumb, till then in its old position, leaves its key and is placed under the 3d finger, while the 2d finger is preparing and striking E. As the 2d finger strikes, the 3d is raised while the thumb is brought from under the hand and prepared on C without changing the position of the hand. The thumb strikes, is shifted forward on its key, the hand is rapidly turned inward, 3d and 2d fingers passing over, etc This is to be repeated until the last octave to be played is reached, when the hand, until then turned inward, is returned to the position for commencing the ascending arpeggio (Fig. 14).

After the first turn of the wrist, the arm is the principal agent in the forward and backward movement of the arpeggios.

Descending arpeggios are to be practised in all keys, styles of touch, and degrees of strength. Practise in slow time at first.

III. PRELIMINARY STUDIES FOR VELOCITY AND EQUALIZATION OF THE FINGERS IN DESCENDING ARPEGGIOS.

Right Hand.

All these examples are to be transposed into all keys.

3. und 2., Vorbereiten des 3. auf G und Anschlag desselben. Der Daumen, der bisher liegen geblieben war, verlässt seine Taste und bewegt sich unter den 3. Finger, während sich der 2. auf E vorbereitet und anschlägt. Mit Anschlag des 2. erhebt sich der 3. und rückt der Daumen auf C zur Vorbereitung, ohne die Hand aus ihrer Lage zu bringen. Anschlag, Schieben auf seiner Taste, rascher Ruck der Hand, Ueberlegen des 3. und 2., etc., etc. Fortsetzung dieses Vorganges bis an das Ende der Arpeggien, wo mit Anschlag des Daumens auf dem letzten C die bisher nach innen gekehrte Hand in jene Lage versetzt wird, welche die Vorbereitung der aufwärtsgehenden Arpeggien bildet.

Nach der ersten Handgelenksdrehung übernimmt der Arm die führende Bewegung in den fortlaufenden Arpeggien.

Die abwärtsgehenden Arpeggien sind wieder in allen Tonarten, Anschlagsweisen und Stärkegraden, sowie vorläufig in langsamem Tempo zu üben.

III. VORSTUDIEN ZUR EGALISIERUNG UND ZUM SCHNELLSPIELEN DER ARPEGGIEN.

Rechte Hand.

Sämtliche Uebungen sind nach dem Muster des Beispieles 76 auszuführen.

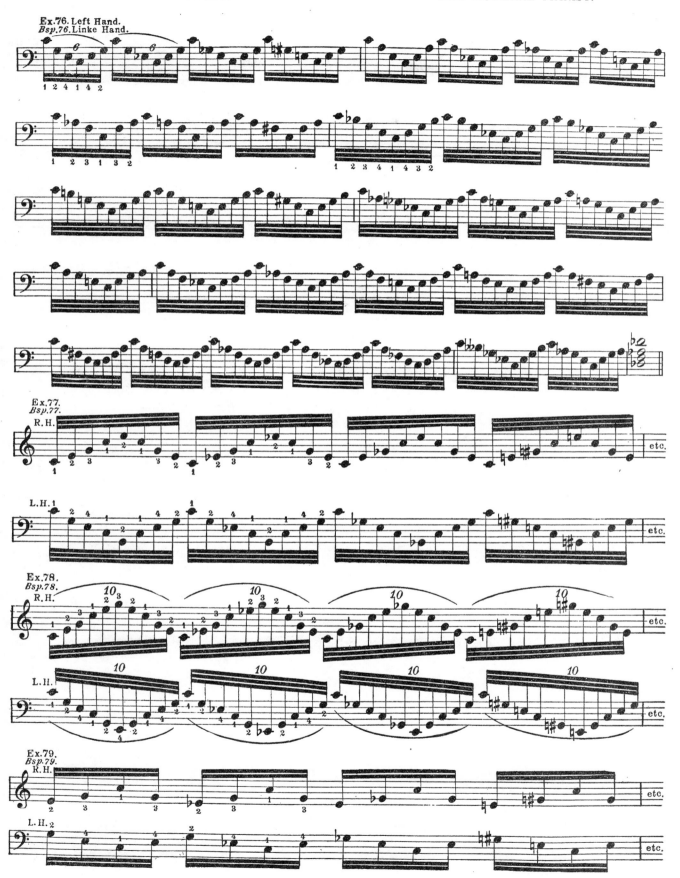

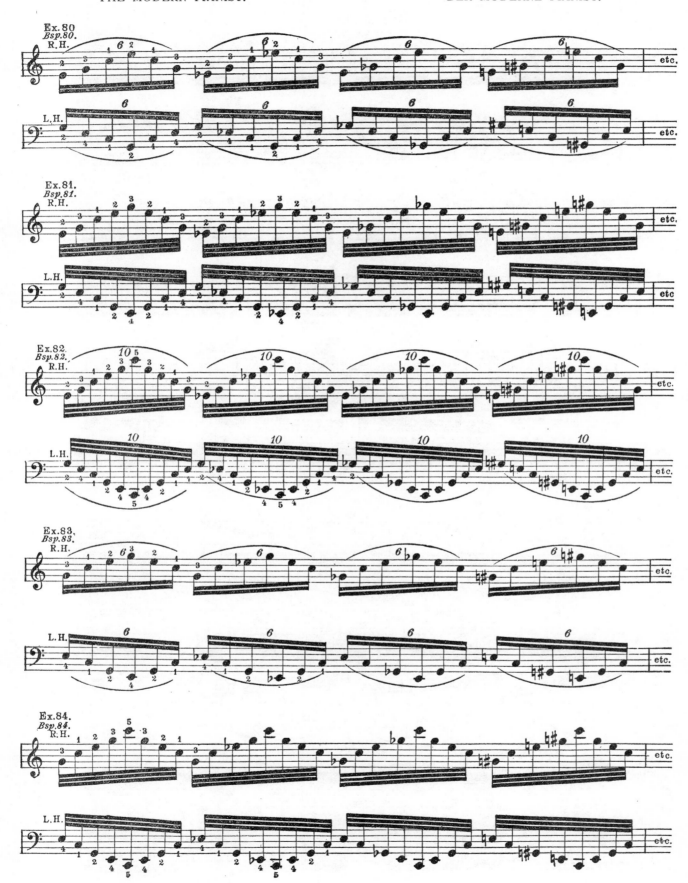

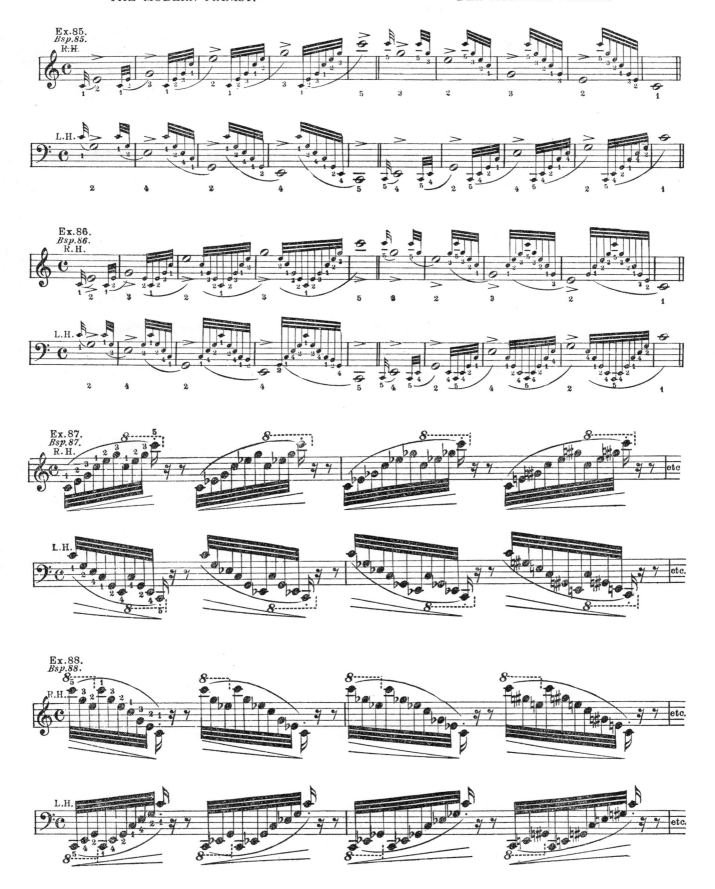

57

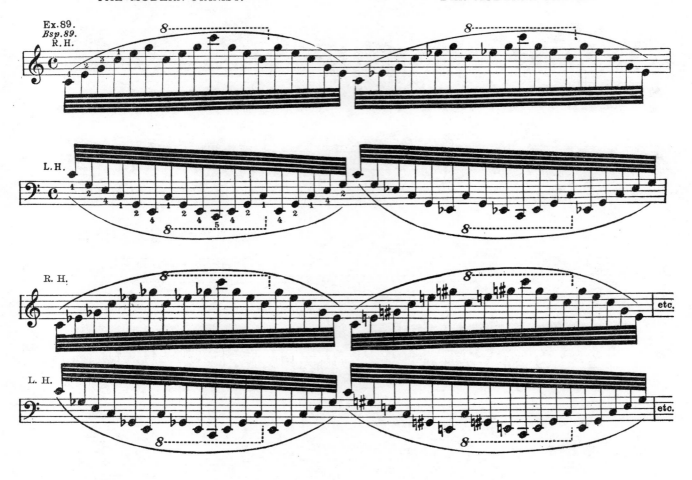

CHAPTER VIII.
DOUBLE NOTES.
THIRDS. SIXTHS.

Great care must be taken that double notes are struck in such a way that their unison does not suffer the slightest break and that the upper note is emphasized more than the lower one. Were this relative strength of the two notes to be reversed, the proper sound effect would be greatly injured. This is particularly to be feared in the right hand, where the 4th finger, by nature the weakest, frequently has the treble note. The upper note should therefore be practised alone with a strong firm touch, while the finger belonging to the lower note accompanies it silently at its distance of thirds and sixths. Particular attention must be paid the 4th finger, that it be well curved, and it is a good thing to strengthen this finger by means of marked accentuation every time it is used. The trill in thirds and sixths should be practised before the diatonic and chromatic scales.

KAPITEL VIII.
DOPPELGRIFFE.
TERZEN. SEXTEN.

Vor allem anderen achte man darauf, die Doppelgriffe so anzuschlagen, dass ihr Zusammenklang nicht die geringste Brechung erleidet und dass die Oberstimme die Unterstimme etwas übertönt. Das Umgekehrte in letzterer Hinsicht würde die richtige Klangwirkung sehr beeinträchtigen. Es ist besonders in der rechten Hand zu befürchten, da hier der 4. Finger, der von Natur bekanntlich schwächste, sehr häufig in der führenden Oberstimme vorkommt. Daher übe man die Oberstimme allein und sehr kräftig, während die Finger der Unterstimme in genauer Distanzeinhaltung von Terz und Sexte stumm mitgehen. Man sehe dabei besonders auf die schön gebogene Haltung des 4. Fingers, und ist es gut, denselben anfänglich bei seinem jemaligen Erscheinen durch bedeutende Accentuirung zu stärken. Zuerst übe man den Terzen- und Sextentriller und gehe dann zu der diatonischen und chromatischen Skala über.

In order to play a scale of thirds as legato as possible, the right hand in the ascending and the left hand in the descending scale should be turned somewhat outward.

Example 90.— Holding the knuckles high and with well-curved fingers, in spite of the somewhat crooked position of the hand, strike C and E with the thumb and 3d finger, while the 2d and 4th fingers are prepared on D and F. At the instant that these strike, the thumb disappears under the hand, and the 3d and 5th fingers are prepared on G and E. After these fingers have struck, the 5th finger remains firmly on G, while the 3d, leaving its key, moves quite close to the keyboard on to A, while at the same time the thumb is prepared on F (see Fig. 19).

Um eine Terzenskala möglichst gebunden zu spielen, halte man die rechte Hand bei der aufwärtsgehenden, die linke Hand bei der abwärtsgehenden Skala etwas nach auswärts geneigt.

Bei Hochhaltung der Mittelhandknöchel und trotz der etwas schiefen Handlage stark gebogenen Fingern, beginne man in Beispiel 90 (rechte Hand) mit Daumen und 3. auf C und E anzuschlagen, während sich 2. und 4. auf D und F vorbereiten. Im Moment, wo diese beiden Finger anschlagen, verschwindet der Daumen unter die Hand und bereiten sich 3. und 5. auf E und G vor. Nach Anschlag dieser Finger bleibt der 5. fest auf G liegen, während der 3., seine Taste verlassend, ganz nahe über die Tastatur auf A rückt, wobei sich gleichzeitig der Daumen auf F vorbereitet (siehe Fig. 19); nun schlagen diese beiden Finger an und

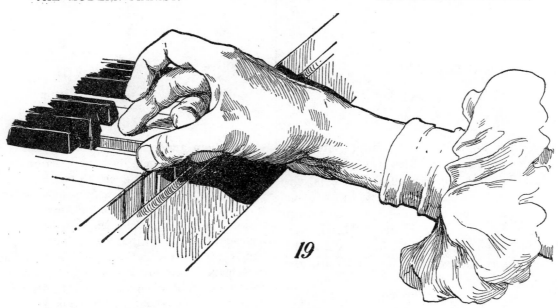

These two fingers then strike while the 2d and 4th are prepared on G and B; as they strike, the 3d finger is moved across the 4th quite close to the keyboard and prepared on C; this brings the thumb under the 2d finger into position on A. The same rules hold in extending the scale, the elbow being kept as much as possible opposite the notes played.

The hand is turned slightly inward in playing the descending scale of thirds with the right hand, as well as the ascending one with the left hand. Great care must be taken in passing over the 4th and 2d or 5th and 3d across the 3d and 1st fingers. If the 4th finger falls upon a black key in striking the 4th and 2d, the hand must make a pretty thorough turn to ensure the 3d and 1st, and 4th and 2d sounding as one; if the 4th finger falls upon a white key it can be "prepared" under the 3d without any turn of the hand. In passing the 5th and 3d over the 3d and 1st the thumb must help in keeping the notes strictly legato.

The same rules apply in scales of the sixths. Here, too, it is only by skill in "passing under" and "passing over" of the fingers that the utmost possible legato is to be gained. Scales of thirds and sixths may, however, be practised staccato as well as in different degrees of strength, with or without preparation, according to the rules given in Chapter II, Touch, *d, e.*

währenddem bereiten sich 2. und 4. auf G und H vor, bei ihrem Anschlag hat sich der 3. ganz nahe an der Tastatur über den 4. bewegt, sich auf C vorbereitend, wobei der Daumen unter dem 2. auf A zu stehen kommt. Die bisher angegebene Art der Ausführung wird durch die weitere Skala unter Mitschieben des Armes angewendet.

Die abwärtsgehende Terzenskala der rechten Hand, sowie die aufwärtsgehende der linken Hand. ist mit einer leichten Wendung der Hand nach innen auszuführen und grosse Vorsicht bei dem Ueberlegen von 4/2 oder 5/3 über 3/1 zu gebrauchen. Fällt der 4. bei dem Terzengriff 4/2 auf eine Obertaste, so muss die Hand eine ziemlich grosse begleitende Drehung mitmachen, um die Bindung zwischen 3/1 und 4/2 aufrecht zu erhalten; fällt der 4. auf eine weisse Taste, so kann er sich ohne Drehung der Hand unter den 3. auf seiner Taste vorbereiten. Bei dem Ueberlegen von 5/3 über 3/1 muss durch den Daumen streng gebunden werden.

Ueber die Haltung der Hand in Sextentonleitern gilt das Gleiche wie in Terzenskalen. Auch hier ist nur durch die Geschicklichkeit des Untersetzens und Ueberlegens der Finger die möglichste Bindung hervorzubringen. Terzen- und Sextenskalen mögen aber auch staccato mit oder ohne Vorbereitung, d. h. nach dem Muster des Kapitels II (Der Anschlag) *d* und *e*, in verschiedenen Stärkegraden geübt werden.

THE MAJOR SCALES.
DUR - SKALEN.

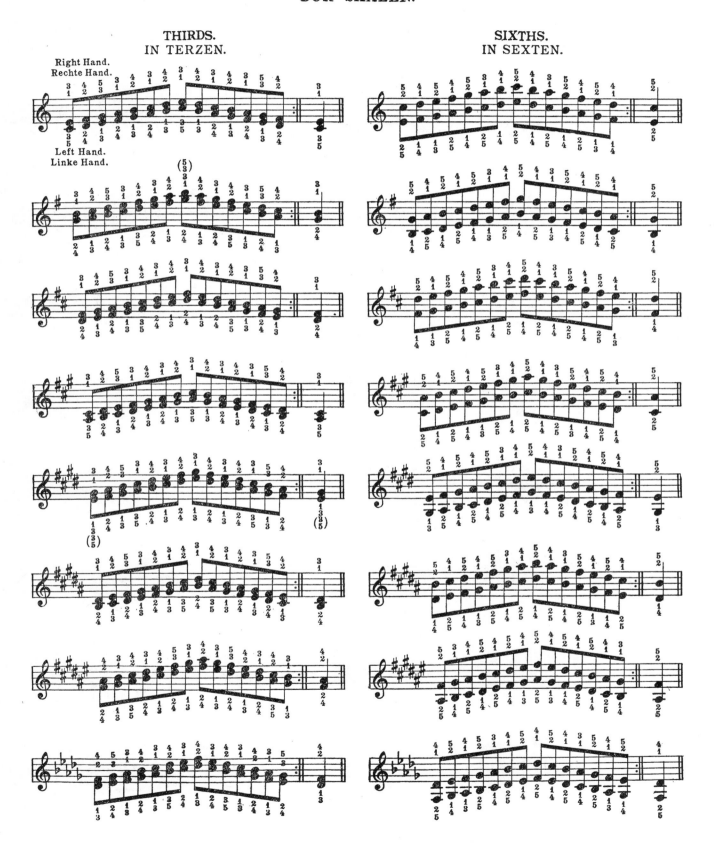

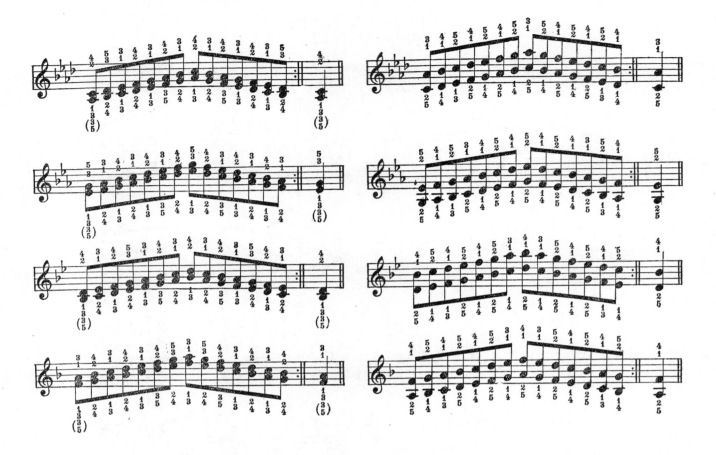

THE MINOR SCALES.
MOLL-SKALEN.

THIRDS.
IN TERZEN.

SIXTHS.
IN SEXTEN.

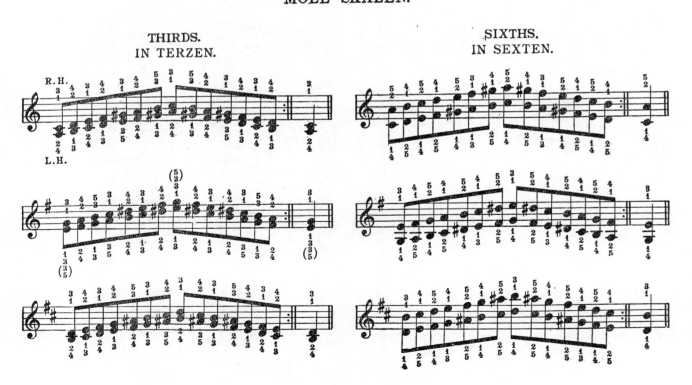

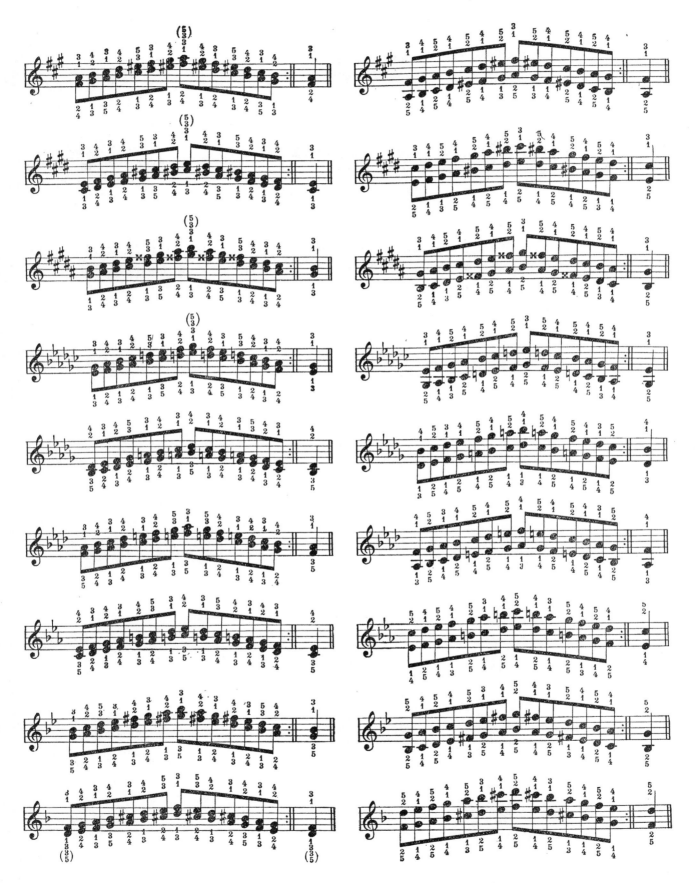

63

THE CHROMATIC SCALE.
CHROMATISCHE SCALA.

DOUBLE THIRDS.
IN TERZEN.

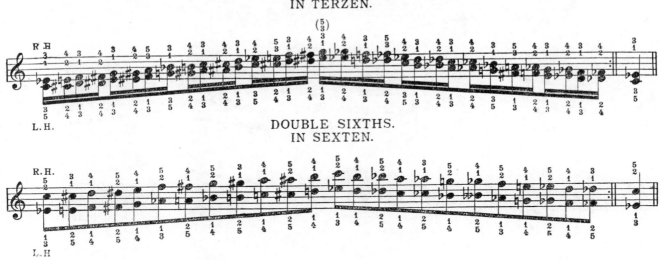

DOUBLE SIXTHS.
IN SEXTEN.

CHAPTER IX.

TO STRETCH A SMALL HAND.

A contracted stretch is one of the greatest hindrances to the acquirement of a brilliant technique. A small hand can, however, with absolute certainty be aided in gaining a normal stretch by the making use of the combined exercises intended for this purpose, always with great caution, and without falling into the error of over-hurrying and over-exertion, dividing the practice through several days, and during small intervals of time. The sum of these exercises is to be repeated and repeated until the desired result is attained.

The exercises of Chapter I (Fig. I), 1st, 2d, and 3d positions, with their stretches between the 2d and 3d, 3d and 4th, and 4th and 5th fingers, coupled to the chord exercises in Chapter VI, form the beginning of this study, and these are of great effect when practised with a correct touch in slow tempo, the hand and fingers being held in perfect position. After this may begin the cultivation of a larger stretch between the thumb and the 2d finger, to be commenced by "preparing" the thumb on C and the 2d finger on C sharp. R. H.

KAPITEL IX.

DEHNUNGSMITTEL FÜR EINE KLEINE HAND.

Der Mangel an genügender Spannweite ist eines der grössten Hindernisse zur Erlangung einer brillanten Technik. Einer kleinen Hand kann man mit Gewissheit zur normalen Spannung verhelfen, wenn man mit grosser Vorsicht, ohne sich im mindesten auf Uebereilung oder Uebertreibung einzulassen, die diesem Zweck entsprechenden Uebungen zusammenstellt, die Verarbeitung des Stoffes auf mehrere Tage einteilt und in kleinen Zeitintervallen mit mehrmaliger Wiederholung im Tage durchnimmt. Der Cyklus dieser Uebungen ist so lange immer wieder vorzunehmen, bis das erwünschte Ziel erreicht ist.

Die Aufstellung und Uebungen der Finger (Fig. I) I., 2. und 3 Stellung mit ihren Dehnungen zwischen 2. und 3. Finger, 3. und 4., 4. und 5., dann die Uebungen in Accordstellung (siehe Kap. VI), machen den Anfang dieses Studiums und sind bei besonders korrekter Hand- und Fingerhaltung, sowie mit genauestem Anschlag zuerst in langsamem Tempo geübt, von grosser Wirkung. Darauf schreite man zur Ausbildung der Vergrösserung des Zwischenraumes vom Daumen zu dem 2. Finger, und beginne in diesem Falle mit der Aufstellung des Daumens auf C und des 2. auf Cis. R. H.

Ex. 91.
Bsp. 91.

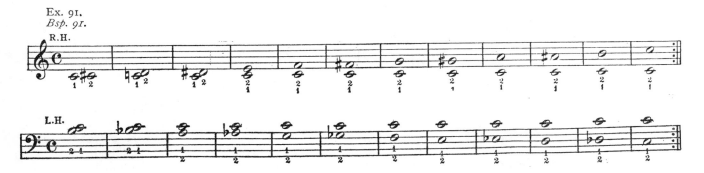

Example 91. R. H.—As can be seen by this example, the thumb keeps the C while the 2d finger strikes in chromatic progression an ever-increasing interval up the octave. In order to obtain the greatest possible result from this growing stretch, the position of the fingers must be that used in the chromatic scale (see Chap. IV). Should the knuckles be held as high as is possible, the consequent lengthening of the distance between the thumb and the 2d finger will most successfully increase the stretch capacity to the utmost limit.

One should strive to keep the high position of the knuckles, even in the intervals of sixth, seventh, and

Beispiel 91. R. H.—Wie man aus dem hier angegebenen Beispiel ersieht, schlägt der Daumen immer wieder seine Taste C an, während der 2. Finger gleichzeitig-anschlagend in chromatischer Tonfolge bis in die Oktave hinauf durch das stets grösser werdende Intervall die auch grösser werdende Dehnung hervorruft. Um das denkbar günstigste Resultat zu erzielen, muss die Aufstellung der Finger nach dem Muster der chromatischen Skala (siehe Kap. IV) erfolgen und sollen die Mittelhandknöchel möglichst hoch gehalten werden, wodurch die Trennung des Daumens und 2. Fingers auf das intensivste erwirkt wird.

Bei den letzten Intervallen, wie Sexte, Septime und

octave, although this will of course be more or less difficult through the necessary flattening of the 2d finger.

The octave stretch once gained, octaves are to be played up and down in chromatic sequence by the thumb and 2d finger.

Oktave, ist durch die notwendige Streckung des 2. Fingers das Emporhalten der Mittelhandknöchel wohl anzustreben, doch in bedeutend geringerem, dieser Lage entsprechendem Masse auszuführen.

Die nun erreichte Oktavespannung des Daumens und des 2. Fingers spiele man in chromatischer Reihenfolge langsam auf und ab.

Ex. 92.
Bsp. 92.

Exercises 91 and 92 are to be practised with the thumb and 3d and thumb and 4th fingers as well.

To stretch the hand further the same exercise must be practised with the 2d and 5th fingers.

Die Uebungen in den Beispielen 91 und 92 sind auch mit dem Daumen und 3. und Daumen und 4. Finger in gleicher Weise auszuführen.

Als weitere Fortsetzung zur Dehnung der Hand ist die Ausbildung der Spannung zwischen 2. und 5. Finger vorzunehmen.

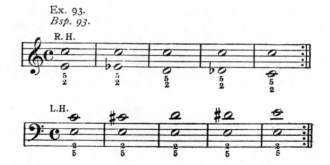

Ex. 93.
Bsp. 93.

Example 93. R. H.—Place 2d and 5th fingers on E and C, the knucklesheld as high as possible, the hand turned somewhat outward. As the 5th finger strikes and re-strikes, the 2d finger moves by chromatic sequence down the octave. This is to be played up and down.

After this, practise with both a raised and lowered wrist, strictly legato, the diatonic and chromatic octave scales, using the fingering given in Kullak's "School of Octave Playing." The diatonic and chromatic scales in sixths (Chap. VIII) are an excellent means of further stretching the hand. The following exercise (94) in double notes and based on the chord sequence found in Chapter VI, is to be transposed into all the different keys.

Beispiel 93. R. H.—Der 2. und 5. Finger stehen auf E und C; die Mittelhandknöchel sind wieder möglichst hoch, die Hand etwas nach auswärts gewendet zu halten. Während des stets auf C au. geführten Anschlages des 5. bewegt sich der 2. mitanschlagend in chromatischer Tonfolge abwärts bis in die Oktave. Nach Erreichung derselben spiele man sie wieder in chromatischer Tonfolge auf und ab.

Darauf übe man in strengster Legatoausführung die diatonischen und chromatischen Oktavenskalen mit dem in Kullak's "Schule des Oktavenspieles" angegebenen Fingersatz, und Vorteil des Hoch- und Tiefhaltens des Handgelenkes. Aus dem vorherigen Kapitel (VIII) wiederhole man die diatonischen und chromatischen Sextentonleitern, welche gleichfalls ein sehr gutes Dehnungsmittel sind. Folgende auf der Accordreihe (siehe Kap. VI) basierende Uebung in Doppelgriffen (94) ist in alle Tonarten zu übertragen: man spiele sie zuerst mit Liegenlassen, dann mit Aufheben der Finger:

Ex.94.
Bsp.94.

Eventually one may cautiously stretch a ninth and then a tenth, holding the distance for a moment or two. The following example, the 5th finger striking *fortissimo*, serves as a good preliminary exercise, and is to be played both legato and staccato (see Ex. 95 and 96).

Endlich spanne man vorsichtig die None, aus dieser die Dezime, indem man bei liegenlassendem Daumen den 5. Finger auf die Nebentaste streckt und diese Spannung eine Weile hält. Das folgende Beispiel bei *ff* Anschlag des 5. Fingers dient als besondere Vorübung dazu und ist teils mit Liegenlassen, teils mit Staccato-Anschlag desselben auszuführen (siehe Bsp. 95 und 96):

Ex. 95.
Bsp. 95.

Ex. 96.
Bsp. 96.

The tenth in unison is developed from these broken tenths after exact observance of the rules given and after many months of study.

Aus diesen gebrochenen Dezimen entwickelt sich der Zusammenklang der Dezime, welcher nach genauester Befolgung und Durchführung alles in diesem Kapitel Gesagten und mehrmonatlichem Studium desselben zu erreichen ist.

CHAPTER X.
OCTAVES.

To impress *the feel* of an octave stretch and the form it necessitates in the hand, is the most important point in octave playing (see Chapter on Chords). Prepare the thumb and 5th finger on the extreme outer edges of the keys R. H., so that the hand is stretched as wide as possible. The thumb lies curved and on its point, the 5th more stretched out. The middle knuckles are raised as high as possible, though of necessity not so high as in a five-finger exercise. The unemployed fingers are lifted high above the keyboard so as to avoid their causing any other note to sound.

The octave form thus unequivocally impressed on the hand, the octave should be struck distinctly, and the hand, with perfect immobility of the arm, raised and bent back as far as possible from the wrist while one counts from 1 to 4 (see Fig. 20). That the fingers keep unchanged the position measured out to them by the octave, while they are in the air, is the main point of this exercise.

After bending the hand back, drop it quickly on to the keyboard, keeping it there for a moment's rest before repeating the exercise.

KAPITEL X.
OKTAVEN.

Was die Oktave anbelangt, so gilt es in erster Linie der Hand ihre Form einzuprägen. Man bereite Daumen und 5. Finger an dem äussersten Rande der Tasten R. H. in deren äussersten Ecken vor, so dass sich die Hand so weit als möglich ausdehnt. Der Daumen liegt gebogen und auf der Spitze, der 5. Finger mehr gestreckt Die Mittelhandknöchel sind so hoch wie möglich, natürlich nicht so hoch wie in einer Fünffingerübung erhoben Die unbeteiligten Finger hebe man weit von der Tastatur auf, damit sie keine anderen Töne miterklingen machen.

Die auf diese Weise sehr auspegrägt gehaltene Oktave schlage man deutlich an und hebe die Hand (siehe Fig. 20), ohne den Arm zu rühren, unter langsamem Zählen von 1 bis 4 empor, bis sie sich so weit als möglich aus dem Handgelenk zurückbiegt. Eine Hauptsache dabei ist die Festhaltung der auf der Tastatur abgemessenen Form durch die nach Verlassen der Tasten unverändert bleibende Haltung der Finger. Nach dem Zurückbiegen der Hand falle man mit dieser schnell auf die Tastatur, verweile auf derselben einige Augenblicke und wiederhole diese Uebung mehrere Male.

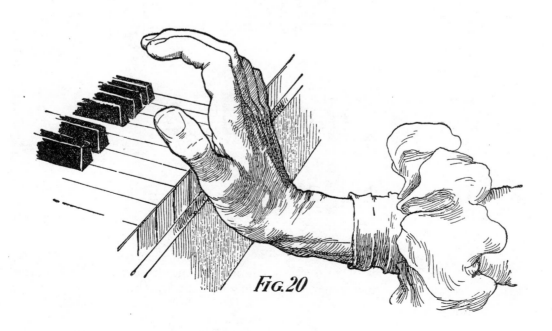

Fig. 20

Octaves played from the wrist are mostly used in quick *p* passages, while quick *f* octave passages, for the sake of strength and steadiness, are played with a high wrist and the slightest possible raising of the hand from the keys, that is, by a close gliding over them.

Particular drilling must be given the wrist by practising the octave on one degree of the staff, following this by the alternation of two degrees, for instance C and D, etc. (see Ex. 97 and 98).

Die Handgelenksoktaven sind meistens bei schnellen *p*-Stellen anzuwenden, während schnelle *f*-Oktavenpassagen, der Kraftentwicklung und Ausdauer wegen, mit hoch aufgestelltem Handgelenk unter geringstem Erheben der Hand von den Tasten, nämlich durch nahes Schieben über dieselben, auszuführen sind.

Besondere Aufmerksamkeit schenke man dem Handgelenk und übe dasselbe durch das Spielen der Oktave auf ein und derselben Tonstufe; darauf mit Abwechslung zweier Tonstufen; z. B. C und D, oder C und Des, etc. (siehe Bsp. 97 und 98).

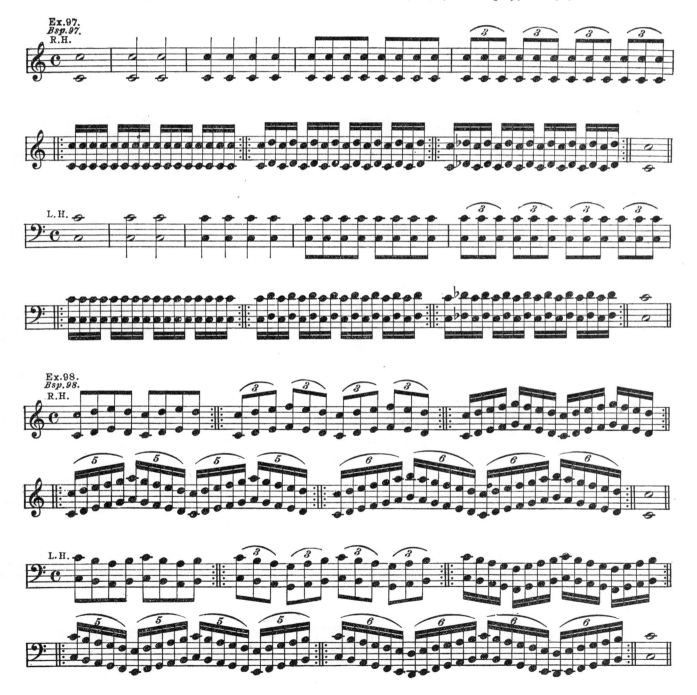

Ex. 100.   Right Hand.
Bsp. 100.   Rechte Hand.

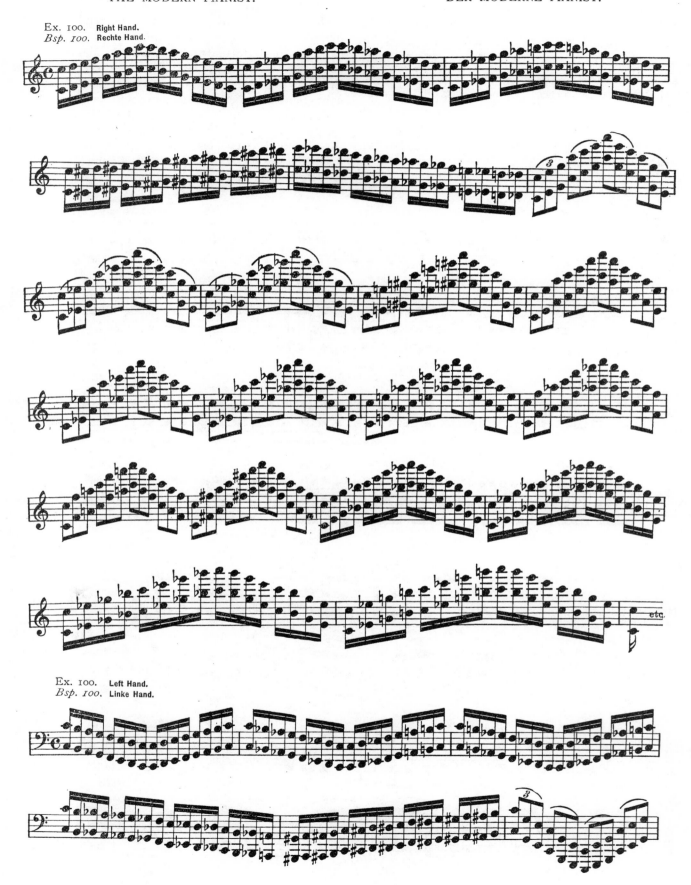

Ex. 100.   Left Hand.
Bsp. 100.   Linke Hand.

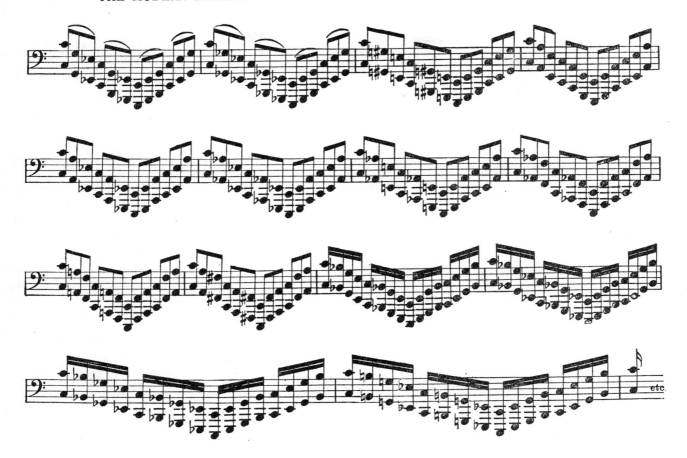

This exercise is also to be carrried out according to the model in exercise 62, Chapter VI : and transposed into all keys.

According to the size of the hand, either the 4th or 5th finger may be used on the black keys in octave playing. For strengthening the single fingers, particularly the 5th, raise the finger, the thumb stationary, while counting slowly from 1 to 4, so high that it at last stands with the whole hand perpendicularly above the thumb, which in the meantime has only made a slight turn inward; it then drops strongly and rapidly, back on its key, without bending at the joints. This exercise should be repeated many times, not only with the 5th finger but the 4th and thumb as well, the thumb being drilled while the 5th or 4th is held down.

All that may be further needed for the development of one's octaves is to be found in Kullak's valuable "School of Octave Playing" (see Introduction). Broken octaves are played not only with the fingers but also with a slight motion of the arm.

Weitere Ausführung nach den Harmonien des Bsp. 62 (Accordgruppe) in Kap. VI: "Der Accord" und Übertragung in alle Tonarten.

Bei den Oktaven auf Obertasten verwende man je nach Grösse der Hand den 4. oder 5. Finger. Zur Stärkung der einzelnen Finger, zuerst des 5., hebe man denselben während ununterbrochenen Liegens des Daumens auf seiner Taste, unter langsamem Zählen von 1 bis 4 so hoch auf, dass er mit der ganzen Hand senkrecht über den Daumen zu stehen kommt, welcher nur eine leichte Wendung nach innen mitgemacht hat; der 5. fällt dann mit grösster Energie und schnellster Bewegung, ohne einzuknicken, mit der Spitze auf seine Taste zurück. Mehrmalige Wiederholung dieser Uebung. Gleiches Vorgehen mit 4. und auch Daumen, letzterer bei Haltung des 5. oder 4. Fingers.

Alles Weitere zur Ausbildung des Oktavenspieles befindet sich in Kullak's vortrefflicher Schule (siehe Einleitung). Gebrochene Oktaven spiele man nicht nur mit den Fingern, sondern wende die leichte Beweglichkeit des Armes an.

ADVICE FOR MUSICAL PERFORM-ANCE.

PART II.

CHAPTER I.

THE STUDY OF BACH'S AND HANDEL'S COMPOSITIONS REGARDING THEIR EFFECT ON TECHNIQUE AND EXECUTION.

As in the previous chapter Kullak's "School of Octave Playing" was made use of, so now should follow in succession those "studies" mentioned in the Introduction: Czerny's "Art of Finger Dexterity", Op. 740, with the complement of that work; Czerny's "Exercises for the Left Hand", Czerny's incomparable, "40 Daily Exercises", Tausig-Ehrlich's "Daily Studies", Clementi's "Gradus ad Parnassum". These works in connection with the exercises contained in this book, will furnish the material for a proper development of technique.

Since modern pianoforte technique demands a classic foundation the study of the compositions of Bach and Handel should, above all others, receive careful attention, as, without these, irreparable deficiencies will make themselves apparent.

Not only for the composer but also for the performer is the art of Bach and Handel equally indispensable. The clear, intelligent performance which Bach's Preludes and Fugues as well as Handel's Suites demand, produces a style of playing which, full of color, cultivates equally the ten fingers.

The flowing style which prevails in most of them tends to perfect the legato playing; the polyphonic analysis necessary for the clear presentation of the independent parts strengthens, through the simultaneous movement of two or more different voices, the individual as well as independent force of each finger. The imperceptible alternation of the hands, the inconvenient progressions and stretches without cover of the pedal, the soundless change of fingers upon a key, all in the quickest possible time,—all this tends to make the fingers extremely dexterous and lissome.

After mastering easily intelligible compositions, such as Bach's charming "French Suites" and "Inventions," also a considerable number of the Preludes and Fugues from the colossal "Wohltemperierte Klavier" must be worked up to the highest possible perfection. This should be done not only for the pro-

RATSCHLÄGE FÜR DEN MUSIKALI-SCHEN VORTRAG.

ZWEITE ABTEILUNG.

KAPITEL I.

DAS STUDIUM BACH'SCHER UND HÄNDEL'-SCHER KOMPOSITIONEN IN BEZUG AUF TECHNIK UND VORTRAG.

Sowie im vorigen Kapitel die Schule des Oktavenspieles von Kullak, so kommen nun der Reihe nach die in der Einleitung genannten Studienwerke in Anwendung: Czerny's Kunst der Fingerfertigkeit, Op. 740, die dazu notwendige Ergänzung: Czerny's Schule der linken Hand, Op. 399, Czerny's unübertreffliche 40 tägliche Uebungen, Op. 337, Taussig-Ehrlich's "Tägliche Studien," Clementi's Gradus ad Parnassum. Diese Werke in Vereinbarung mit allem bisher in diesem Buche Gesagten müssen die richtige Entwicklung der Technik zur Folge haben.

Da auch die modernste Technik einer klassischen Grundlage bedarf, so unternehme man vor allem anderen das Studium Bach'scher und Händel'scher Kompositionen, da sich ohne dasselbe unverbesserliche Mängel fühlbar machen würden.

Nicht allein dem schaffenden, auch dem darstellenden Musiker ist Bach'sche sowie Händel'sche Kunst unentbehrlich. Der klare, verständnisvolle Vortrag, welchen Bach'sche Präludien und Fugen, gleichwie Händel'sche Suiten erfordern, erzeugt ein klangreiches, die Gleichmässigkeit aller zehn Finger ausbildendes Spiel.

Der gebundene Stil, der in den meisten vorherrscht, ruft die Vollendung des Legato hervor; die polyphone Arbeit, welche Verfolgung und plastische Klarlegung der einzelnen selbstständigen Stimmen, sowie deutliches Zusammenerklingen erfordert, wirkt sehr kräftigend auf den Anschlag des einzelnen Fingers. Das unmerkliche Abwechseln der Hände, das manchmal sehr unbequeme Greifen und Spannen ohne verdeckendes Pedal, das oftmalige stumme Wechseln der Finger auf einer Taste, alles in zumeist schnellem Tempo, macht die Finger höchst geschickt und geschmeidig.

Nach Ausführung leichter verständlicher Kompositionen, z. B. der reizvollen *französischen Suiten* und *Inventionen* von Bach, etc., muss aus dem Kolossalwerk des *wohltemperierten Klavieres* zum mindesten eine Anzahl von Präludien und Fugen bis zu möglichster Vollendung durchgearbeitet werden. Es geschehe dies sowohl zur Beförderung der Technik, als auch zur Läuterung des Geschmackes.

motion of technique but also for refinement of taste.

No one, not even the warmest admirer of the modern school, should neglect studying deeply, for a time at least, the works of the great classic composers, giving particularly to J. S. Bach and G. F. Handel their wonted and well-deserved places of honor. These names are inscribed with eternal letters in the history of music; they will endure so long as music endures and shine forever as guiding beacons to every true and worthy school of production and reproduction!

CHAPTER II.

RHYTHM.

An indispensable attribute of good pianoforte playing is Rhythm. It is of great advantage to be gifted by nature with this sense; for although its artificial attainment is possible, the task presents peculiar difficulties.

Experience has taught that counting aloud is one of the most successful means for combating rhythmical defects. A decided "holding back" at the last part of a bar, in order to prevent precipitation in reaching the first beat of the next, successfully counteracts the disturbance in time which the constantly increasing haste, and the senseless scrambling, of some players creates. From this "holding back," exercised at first with deliberation, one gradually develops the equableness and solidity necessary to the time sense. The help of the metronome is also of value. To play etudes and pieces in the most varied degrees of velocity, accompanied by the occasional beat of this instrument, is a necessity; especially if one tries afterward to render from memory the various tempos as exactly as possible without this assistance. The conventional hurrying in *forte* and slackening in the *piano* passages indulged in by players lacking a decided sense of rhythm, has a particularly amateurish sound; to give one's playing breadth and swing, the exact opposite should be the rule. There are, however, exceptional cases in which an accelerando accompanies a *ff*, and a ritenuto a *pp*.

An accelerando or a ritenuto occurring in one or several bars must be brought back to time in so artistic a manner that neither the one nor the other is in any way conspicuous. Like notes, pauses demand equal care and consideration, and are to be given their full value.

Under the heading to this chapter the various dance rhythms must also be considered: the waltz, polonaise, mazurka, gavotte, menuet, etc. The pianist should thoroughly investigate for himself their peculiarities, rendering them with the utmost exactness, retaining, if possible, the characteristics of race and the period of time to which they belong.

Niemand, auch jener welcher der modernsten Richtung huldigt, versäume, sich wenigstens eine Zeit lang in die Werke der Klassiker zu vertiefen und namentlich J. S. Bach und G. F. Händel die wohlverdienten und altgewohnten Ehrenplätze einzuräumen. Diese Namen sind mit ewigen Lettern in die Geschichte der Musik eingeschrieben; sie werden bestehen, so lange sie besteht und werden stets jeder tieferen Richtung musikalischer Produktion und Reproduktion wegweisend voranleuchten!

KAPITEL II.

RHYTHMUS.

Eine Hauptbedingung guten Klavierspieles ist der Rhythmus. Von grossem Vorteil ist der von Natur verliehene Besitz rhythmischen Gefühles; die künstliche Erlangung desselben ist wohl erreichbar, bietet aber eine besonders schwierige Aufgabe.

Als erprobtes Mittel zur Bekämpfung rhythmischer Fehler sei *lautes Zählen* angegeben und ein ausgesprochenes *Zurückhalten des letzten Teiles eines Taktes*, um das überaus störende Zufrühkommen auf das Eins des nächsten Taktes zu verhindern; auch dem bei vielen Spielern im Verlauf eines Stückes zunehmenden Hasten, oft geradezu kopflosen Jagen ist dadurch erfolgreich entgegenzuarbeiten. Aus diesem anfänglich mit Bedacht durchgeführten Zurückhalten entwickelt sich später der *gleichmässige Fluss der taktischen Gliederung*. Die Hilfe des Metronoms ist gleichfalls in Anspruch zu nehmen und spiele man Etuden und Stücke in den verschiedensten Schnelligkeitsgraden unter zeitweiligem Mitschlagen desselben; hierauf versuche man ohne dessen Mitwirkung die diversen Tempi aus dem Kopfe genauestens wiederzugeben. Sehr dilletantisch klingt bei Spielern ohne ausgeprägt rhythmische Empfindung das geradezu stereotype Eilen bei *forte*- und Langsamwerden bei *piano*-Stellen; um dem Spiel Breite und Aufschwung zu verleihen, hat gerade das umgekehrte Verfahren die richtige Wirkung. Deshalb sind aber Ausnahmsfälle, in denen sich das *Accelerando* dem *ff*, oder das *Ritenuto* dem *pp* zugesellen, nicht ausgeschlossen.

Eines der wichtigsten Erfordernisse ist es, das in einem oder mehreren Takten stattgehabte *Accelerando* oder *Ritenuto* in dem darauffolgenden Takte oder der darauffolgenden Taktreihe künstlerisch dermassen *einzubringen*, dass weder das eine noch das andere in irgend welcher Art aufgefallen ist. Wie die Noten, so verdienen auch die *Pausen* gleiche Berücksichtigung und sind in Bezug auf ihren Wert strengstens einzuhalten.

In dieses Kapitel schlagen auch die Rhythmen der verschiedenen Tanzweisen ein, wie *Walzer, Polonaise, Mazurka, Gavotte, Menuet*, etc., etc., deren Eigentümlichkeit der Spieler genauestens wiedergeben muss, um der Komposition ihren nationalen und zeitgemässen Charakter zu wahren.

THE MODERN PIANIST.

CHAPTER III.

PEDALING.

The motto for studying the pedal should be, "Rather too little than too much," since the too frequent and continuous use of the pedal undermines clearness by blurring the harmony. The prime requisites for a discriminating use of the pedal are a fine ear and a knowledge of harmony. The pedal can undoubtedly produce fine effects, and is of great advantage in swelling a crescendo, in defining the movement of the various melodies, and connecting separate tones and harmonies.

Notes which can not be connected by the fingers, can be bound together by the foot, through the use of the pedal (see Ex. 9).

DER MODERNE PIANIST.

KAPITEL III.

PEDALISIERUNG.

Bei dem Studium der Pedalisierung gelte die Devise: "*Eher zu wenig als zu viel.*" da der zu oftmalige und zu langanhaltende Gebrauch des Pedales durch Verschwinden der Harmonien die Klarheit untergräbt. Zur richtigen Anwendung des Pedales sind vor allem ein vortreffliches Gehör und die Kenntnisse der Harmonielehre notwendig. Zweifellos bringt das Pedal grosse Wirkungen hervor und ist namentlich auf Steigerung des Klanges, plastisches Hervortreten der Melodien und Bindung der einzelnen Töne und Harmonien von grossem Einfluss.

Was die Finger nicht mehr binden können, bindet oft der Fuss durch die Anwendung des Pedales: (siehe Bsp. 9).

Literature Ex. 9.
Literatur Beispiel 9.

BEETHOVEN, Op. 28.

That treble passages require far more pedal than those in the lower octaves is necessitated by the construction of the piano, whose upper registers, vibrating less, are more in need of binding or connecting by the pedal than the bass with its more sustained tones.

The pedal lends great charm to an ascending scale played crescendo in the treble (see Ex. 10); with

Dass das Pedal in den im Diskant geschriebenen Stellen bedeutend mehr in Anwendung kommt, als in den tieferen Oktaven, ist durch den Bau des Klavieres veranlasst, dessen höhere Lage kürzer klingt und daher der Bindung mehr bedarf als die tiefe mit ihren langgezogenen Tönen.

Der aufwärtsgehenden und zugleich crescendierenden Skala verleiht das Pedal, in der höchsten Lage angewandt, vielen Reiz (siehe Bsp. 10); bei der abwärtsge-

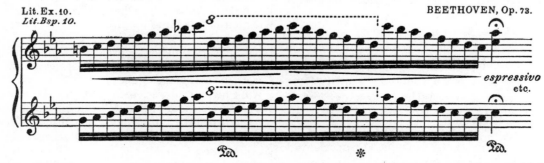

Lit. Ex. 10.
Lit. Bsp. 10.

BEETHOVEN, Op. 73.

a descending scale, for reasons above given, the pedaling must be of short duration (see Ex. 11).

henden sei es nach kurzer Anwendung bald aufgehoben, (siehe Bsp. 11).

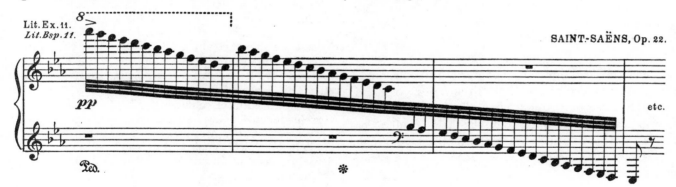

Lit. Ex. 11.
Lit. Bsp. 11.

SAINT-SAËNS, Op. 22.

For the purpose of increasing the strength, the pedal may be held throughout an ascending scale played with great velocity, providing the foot is removed instantaneously with the highest note of the scale. This skilful use of the pedal makes a permissible deception of the hearer, since by quickly leaving off the pedal, its previous use entirely escapes him, especially across the space of a roomy concert hall (see Exs. 12 and 13).

Bei einer im schnellen Tempo aufwärts fliegenden Skala kann das Pedal zum Zwecke der Krafterhöhung ganz durchgehalten werden, wenn es bei der letzten, der höchsten Note der Skala, blitzschnell aufgehoben wird. In dieser geschickten Anwendung liegt eine erlaubte Täuschung für den Hörer; durch das rasche Abziehen des Pedales ist ihm der Gebrauch desselben, besonders im weiten Raume des Konzertsaales, geradezu entgangen (siehe Bsp. 12 und 13).

Lit. Ex. 12.
Lit. Bsp. 12.

CHOPIN, Op. 23.

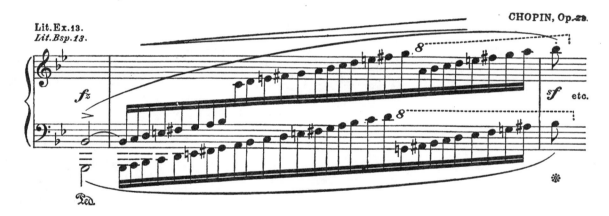

Lit. Ex. 13.
Lit. Bsp. 13.

CHOPIN, Op. 23.

The arpeggios, on account of the notes belonging to the same chord, allow of the uninterrupted use of the pedal in all parts of the piano (see Exs. 14 and 15).

Die Arpeggien mit ihren zusammenhängenden Accordtönen vertragen die ununterbrochene Pedalisierung in allen Lagen des Klavieres (siehe Bsp. 14 und 15).

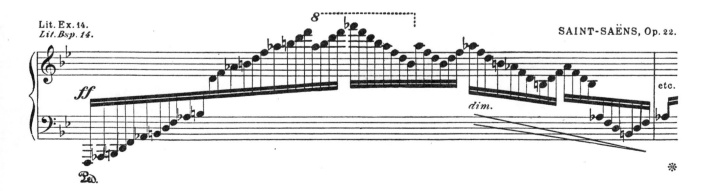

Lit. Ex. 14.
Lit. Bsp. 14.

SAINT-SAËNS, Op. 22.

The pedal is applied sometimes at the same moment with the touch of the fingers, sometimes afterward. With the introduction of a harmony the pedal is pressed simultaneously with the first note; in a sequence of harmonies the foot rises with the striking of a harmony, to come down directly afterward, while the harmony is still in force. This is called the "Syncopated Pedal" (see Lit. Exs. 16, 17, 18).

Im Allgemeinen wird das Pedal bald *mit* dem Anschlag der Finger zugleich, bald *nach* demselben angewendet. Mit dem freien Einsatz der Harmonien setzt das Pedal im gleichen Momente ein; in der Aufeinanderfolge der Harmonien drückt der Fuss erst das Pedal, bis die Finger die nächsten angeschlagen haben, wodurch die grösste Bindung und Reinheit möglich wird; das letztere kann man das *synkopierte Pedal* nennen (siehe Bsp. 16, 17, 18).

A long-sounding bass note makes a long-held pedal possible (see Lit. Ex. 19); while a quick-changing bass only allows of a slight use of the pedal or none at all (see Lit. Ex. 20).

Die langtönende Bassnote ermöglicht ein langklingendes Pedal (siehe Bsp. 19), während der bewegliche Bass nur geringe oder gar keine Pedalisierung zulässt (siehe Bsp. 20).

Lit. Ex. 19.
Lit. Bsp. 19.　　　SCHUMANN, Op. 21, N⁰ 7.

Lit. Ex. 20.
Lit. Bsp. 20　　　SCHUMANN, Op. 21, N⁰ 7.

It is important, in dispersed passages or those requiring a wide stretch, to hold down the bass notes with the pedals before removing the fingers; for otherwise such passages lose their musical basis and sound empty as well as incorrect (see Exs. 21 and 22). The pedal

Schwierig ist es in weitgriffigen Stellen die Bassnoten noch *vor* Verlassen der Finger durch das Pedal festzuhalten; es ist jedoch unumgänglich notwendig, da sonst dieselben der musikalischen Basis entbehren und sowohl leer als auch unrichtig klingen würden (siehe Bsp. 21 und 22). Das Pedal muss, in anderen Worten,

SCHUMANN, Op. 11.

Lit. Ex. 21.
Lit. Bsp. 21.

Lit. Ex. 22.
Lit. Bsp. 22.　　　CHOPIN, Op. 15, N⁰ 1.

must, in other words, catch and hold the bass note or notes before the hand moves on.

Not only the changing harmonies but the melody itself and the tempo govern the use of the pedal. Quick time allows of considerable less pedaling, while slow time requires more.

die Bassnote treffen und festhalten, bevor die Hand zu ihrer weiteren Arbeit übergeht.

Entscheidend für den Pedalgebrauch ist nicht nur der Wechsel der Harmonie, sondern auch die Melodie selbst (siehe Bsp. 23)

Lit. Ex. 23.
Lit. Bsp. 23.　　　SCHUMANN, Op. 11.

Numerous examples might be cited, in which the various uses of the pedal sometimes depend on the change of the harmonies, sometimes on the construction of the melody, sometimes on the gradations of sound from *pp* to *ff*, as well as on a thousand fine shades of taste and feeling. The player who, in everything that presupposes delicate study, uses the pedal in so happy

und endlich das Tempo. Im schnellen Tempo ist bedeutend weniger zu pedalisieren, als im langsamen Tempo.

So gäbe es noch zahlreiche Beispiele anzuführen, deren Pedalbehandlung bald der Wechsel der Harmonien, bald der Bau der Melodien, bald die Klangfarben vom *pp* bis zum *ff* und tausend Nuancen **des**

a manner that it never makes itself obtrusively noticeable, but follows closely and naturally the general phrasing, understands its proper application and knows how to lend his instrument the breath of inspiration. To gain this the player should practice in perfect quiet; he should make long pauses between the passages where pedal is used, letting the sound during this time repeat itself in his head without looking at the music or playing on the instrument; the sound, good and faulty alike, will come back to him like an echo, thus allowing him to decide between the two with certainty.

CHAPTER IV.

THE MELODY AND ITS RULES.

To "sing" on the piano is far more difficult than on any other instrument. The tone produced by a piano is comparatively short, and unlike other instruments permits of no crescendo in the sound when once it has been produced. To mold the melody and make it stand out distinctly from the framework of the piece one must play it with a touch that is firm and strong, yet yielding a tone that is not coarse. The accompaniment, with its weaker gradations, must nevertheless accommodate itself suitably to the rise and fall of the melody.

For the artistic interpretation of a melody there are required not only practised and skilful fingers, well drilled in all kinds of touch, but also a well-developed sense of rhythm, and knowledge of the finer uses of the pedal. The most important rules which can be given as a basis for a musically correct and beautiful rendering of a melody are the following:

1. An ascending series of notes demands a crescendo, its highest note the strongest accent, the descending series of notes a decrescendo.

2. Of two notes the higher is the stronger.

3. Of two notes the longer one is the stronger.

4. The accentuation depends on the time. In common time the principal accent is laid on 1 and 3, in ¾ time on 1, in ⁶⁄₈ time on 1 and 4, etc., etc.

5. When the same note (see Ex. 24, bars 3 and 4) or

Geschmackes, der Empfindung und der Stimmung bedingen. Wer bei alledem, was ein subtiles Studium voraussetzt, das Pedal so glücklich gebraucht, dass es sich niemals aufdrängt, sondern sich in natürlicher Weise der allgemeinen Phrasierung anschmiegt, der versteht das Pedal richtig anzuwenden, der versteht seinem Instrumente beseelenden Atem zu verleihen. Um dies zu erreichen, studiere er in ganz stiller Umgebung, pausiere nach der pedalisierten Stelle eine geraume Weile und lasse dieselbe, ohne das Notenblatt zu besehen oder auf dem Klavier zu spielen, in seinem Kopfe wiedererklingen; echoartig wird ihm Gutes und Fehlerhaftes zurücktönen und sichere Unterscheidung zwischen Beiden ermöglichen.

KAPITEL IV.

DIE MELODIE UND IHRE REGELN.

Auf dem Klaviere zu "singen" ist ungleich schwerer als auf den meisten anderen Instrumenten, da der Klavierton verhältnismässig kurz ist und nach seinem Erklingen kein Anschwellen zulässt. Um die Melodie plastisch aus dem Rahmen des Stückes heraustreten zu lassen, spiele man sie mit möglichst vollem, grossem und doch weichem Anschlage; die Begleitung, welche sich in schwächerer Klangfarbe unterordnet, schmiegt sich aber dennoch in passendster Weise ihrem Aufschwung und Verklingen an.

Für die künstlerische Wiedergabe der Melodie sind noch nebst den in allen Anschlagsarten geschulten und verwendbaren Fingern, das ausgebildete rhythmische Gefühl, sowie die Kenntnisse der feinen Pedalisierung erforderlich. Der musikalisch richtige und schön Vortrag einer Melodie basiert auf mancherlei Gesetzen, von denen die wichtigsten hier angegeben seien.

1. Die aufsteigende Notenreihe erfordert das Crescendo, ihre Spitze den stärksten Accent, die absteigende Notenreihe das Decrescendo.

2. Von zwei Noten ist die höhere die stärkere.

3. Von zwei Noten ist die längere die stärkere.

4. Die Accentuierung wird auch durch die Takteinteilung bestimmt. Im ¼ Takt fallen die Hauptaccente auf 1 und 3, im ¾ Takt auf 1, im ⁶⁄₈ Takt auf 1 und 4, etc.

5. Bei der sofortigen Wiederholung derselben Note (siehe Bsp. 24, 3. und 4. Takt) oder derselben Phrase

Lit. Ex. 24.
Lit. Bsp. 24.

SCHUMANN, Op. 21, No 7.

phrase (see Exs. 25, 26, 27, 28, 29) is repeated the same | (siehe Bsp. 25, 26, 27, 28 und 29) darf nicht der gleiche

Lit. Ex. 29.
Lit. Bsp. 29.   CHOPIN, Op. 15, No 1.

degree of strength in touch must never be used; both the gradations in sound as well as of expression must be intensified (see Exs. 25, 26) or diminished (see Exs. 27, 28); in many cases even the tempo can be slightly varied (see Ex. 29). This infuses life and variety into the melody and avoids any stiffness which can arise from lack of change.

To be sure, there are exceptions to these as to all rules; for example, it is possible, as regards the first, that the climax of an ascending passage should be *piano* instead of *forte* (see Ex. 30).

Stärkegrad im Anschlag angewendet werden, sondern es muss eine Erhöhung (siehe Bsp. 25 und 26) oder Verminderung der Tonfarbe, sowie des Ausdrucks (siehe Bsp. 27 und 28) oft gleichzeitig eine Veränderung des Tempos (siehe Bsp. 29) stattfinden, um jede Härte zu vermeiden und Leben und Abwechslung zu bringen.

Natürlich giebt es auch hier, wie bei allen Regeln, Ausnahmen; z. B. ist es gleich in Betreff der ersten möglich, dass der Höhepunkt der aufsteigenden Notenreihe anstatt des Kraftmomentes eines *p* bedarf: (siehe Bsp. 30).

Lit. Ex. 30.
Lit. Bsp. 30.   SCHUMANN, Op. 11.

As regards rules 2, 3, and 4, there are cases when the lower note has to be played louder than the higher one, either on account of its value (see Ex. 31) or the ac-

Was Nr. 2, 3 und 4 anbelangt, so kann es einen Fall geben, in welchem die tiefere Note entweder durch ihren Wert (siehe Bsp. 31) oder durch den Accent der

Lit. Ex. 31.
Lit. Bsp. 31. **Lento sostenuto.**   CHOPIN, Op. 27, No 2.

centuation of a beat (see Ex. 32), or both together (see Ex. 33).

Takteinteilung (siehe Bsp. 32) oder durch beides zusammen (siehe Bsp. 33) einen *stärkeren* Klang erfordert, als die höheren Noten.

A composer can also expressly denote that stress should be placed on an unaccented beat (see Exs. 34, 35, and 36) or that a crescendo be abruptly broken off,

Auch kann es der durch besondere Markierung bezeichnete spezielle Wunsch des Komponisten sein, den Nebentaktteil mit einem besonderen Accent zu versehen (siehe Bsp. 34, 35 und 36) oder das begonnene

can even direct a repetition of this departure from the rule, (see Ex. 37).

Crescendo ganz plötzlich abzubrechen, selbst **mit** Wiederholung dieses Vorganges (siehe Bsp. 37).

In all these cases rules must be abandoned in order to obey the composer's wishes. When the accompaniment differs entirely in rhythm from the melody, it can only be subordinated through painstaking separate practice until it can be played with perfect smoothness and ease. With careful practice it can be made to sustain the melody without occupying a prominent part (see Ex. 38).

In allen diesen Fällen heisst es die Gesetze zu umgehen und den Einfällen des genialen Tondichters zu folgen. Was noch ausserdem die Begleitung anbelangt, so ist es sehr schwer, ihre Nebenrolle festzuhalten, wenn sie durch eine von der Melodie vollkommen ungleiche Takteinteilung die Aufmerksamkeit zu sehr in Anspruch nehmen würde; durch das auf ihr Studium gerichtete Hauptaugenmerk, durch die dadurch erreichte vollkommene Glätte, wird die Begleitung wieder zur unaufdringlichen, wohlthuenden Nebensache: (siehe Bsp. 38).

Lit. Ex. 38.
Lit. Bsp. 38.

CHOPIN, Op. 58.

Where the accompaniment is divided between the two hands, the interlocking of the passages must take place so imperceptibly that it sounds as though played by one hand only (see Ex. 39).

Ist die Begleitung auf beide Hände verteilt, so muss das Abwechseln der Hände so unmerklich vor sich gehen, als wäre sie von einer Hand gespielt: (siehe Bsp. 39).

Besides the rules and exceptions mentioned, there are numberless varieties of expression and methods of execution which may be called forth by a sudden impulse of the interpreter, which so long as they conform to the laws of beauty will never fail in effect although deviating from the general standard.

Naturally everything said in this chapter about a singing melody or "cantilena" holds equally as well for all themes, even those consisting principally of rhythmic combinations.

Ausser diesen angeführten Regeln und Ausnahmen birgt das reiche Gebiet der Melodie noch unzählige Spielweisen und Ausdrucksarten, welche, wenn auch abweichend von der Norm, durch den momentanen Impuls des Interpreten erst geschaffen werden und, sobald sie den Gesetzen des Schönen entsprechen, ihre Wirkung nicht verfehlen können. Selbstverständlich ist alles über die Melodie Gesagte—hier mehr als gesangsmässig geführte Stimme verstanden—auf sämtliche Themen, auch auf die überwiegend in rhythmische Bewegung aufgehenden, zu übertragen und betrifft auch den musikalischen Vortrag im Allgemeinen.

CHAPTER V.

HOW TO PRACTISE.

How one practises signifies a great deal to the character of the results gained. The standard should be not the immoderate expenditure of time, but how thorough use is made of every moment. As the exhausting path of mechanical practice has injured many a constitution, as many a hand has been strained, so too, have talented pupils sunk into discouragement and even come to grief altogether on account of this check to further progress. The senseless hundredfold repetition of passages, the endless and purposeless playing through of pieces and etudes is therefore utterly to be condemned, since it leads only to a strain of body and mind, of muscles and intellect. The last, which is left pretty much unused by the average pianist, plays the chief part in correct study, and must therefore be kept continually fresh and attentive during the work. In order to prevent any slackening of attention, it is advisable to make the practise periods short and divided from one another by pauses. Having obtained a good general idea of all that has to be done, one should make a well-defined division of the study time, since regularity leads to the best results. Four, or at most five, hours of study, rationally spent every day, are sufficient to attain a genuinely artistic style of playing.

One begins, of course, with technical exercises, taking first five-finger exercises and scales in all degrees of strength and styles of touch. After this follows time spent on some important branch of technique, e. g., the trill, stretches, octaves, etc. During the struggle with some such special difficulty, however, the other divisions of technique must not be neglected, but are to be worked at in proper order so that their development may be uniform. As, at the most, these exercises cannot take up more than one to two hours daily, it will, on account of their number, take several days to go through them; at the end of this time the exercises are to be recommenced and repeated in the same manner.

After these preliminary exercises attention should be turned to the "Etudes," to which the allottment of an hour daily is by no means too much to require of the pianist. It should be remarked here that in the course of several months' study, conducted in this manner, it is advisable to introduce a variation in the regular routine by attempting some difficult passages from etudes and pieces without any technical preparation, performing them at once as perfectly as possible, with all the assistance that the exertion of a strong will can give. This has a definite object: that of giving the pianist the necessary confidence in himself, of obtaining a proof at any given moment, of the knowledge so far acquired of a passage in hand, and not to become the slave of

KAPITEL V.

DIE ART DES STUDIERENS UND AUS-WENDIGLERNENS.

Die *richtige Art zu üben* ist von nicht zu unterschätzender Bedeutung: nicht ein übermässiger Aufwand von Zeit, sondern die gründlichste Ausnützung jedes Augenblickes ist hier massgebend. Wie mancher Organismus hat schon auf dem erschöpfenden Wege des mechanischen Uebens Schaden genommen, wie manche Hand sich überspielt, wie ist auch oftmals ein Talent angesichts stockenden Fortschreitens in Mutlosigkeit versunken, ja sogar daran gescheitert! Das gedankenlose hundertmalige Repetieren fehlerhafter Stellen, das end- und zwecklose Durchspielen von Etuden und Stücken ist daher ganz verwerflich, denn es führt nur zur Abspannung des Körpers und des Geistes, der Muskeln und der Denkkraft. Letztere, welche in den meisten Köpfen der Durchschnittspianisten ziemlich unausgenützt ruht, spielt im richtigen Studium gerade die grösste Rolle und muss deshalb während der Arbeit in steter Frische und Spannung erhalten bleiben. Um ihr Nachlassen zu verhindern, ist es ratsam, das Ueben in *kurzen, durch Pausen getrennten Zeitabschnitten* vorzunehmen. In Uebersicht des ganzen Stoffes mache sich der Studierende eine bestimmte Einteilung der Arbeitszeit zurecht, da die Regelmässigkeit zu bestem Resultat führt. Vier, höchstens fünf Stunden täglichen, mit Verständnis durchgeführten Studiums genügen zur Erreichung eines wahrhaft künstlerischen Spieles. Selbstverständlich beginne man mit den technischen Uebungen, zunächst mit den Fünffinger- und Skalenbewegungen in allen Stärkegraden und Anschlagsarten. Daran schliesse sich die Bearbeitung irgend eines speziell wichtigen Zweiges der Technik, z. B. des Trillers, der Spannungen, Oktaven, etc. Während der Bekämpfung einer solchen Hauptschwierigkeit dürfen aber die anderen Abschnitte der Technik nicht vernachlässigt werden, sondern sind betreffs gleichmässiger Entfaltung derselben in zweckmässiger Anordnung vorzunehmen. Da diese Uebungen nicht mehr als eine, bis höchstens zwei Stunden täglich ausfüllen dürfen, so werden sie sich ihrer Mannigfaltigkeit wegen auf mehrere Studientage erstrecken müssen, nach deren Ablauf der ganze Cyklus zu wiederholen ist.

Nach diesen Vorübungen unternehme man das Studium der Etuden, dem täglich eine Stunde einzuräumen, gewiss keine zu grosse Anforderung an den Spieler ist. Hier sei bemerkt, dass es sehr günstig ist, in der mehrere Monate festgehaltenen Studieneinteilung mit Beginn der technischen Uebungen, eine Veränderung vorzunehmen und zwar versuche man schwierige Stellen aus Etuden und Stücken ohne technische Vorbereitung mit Einsetzen der ganzen Willenskraft sofort in möglichster Vollendung auszuführen.

perpetual preparatory exercises. As, however, no day should pass without technical exercises, these trials may be relegated to the close of the day's work.

The same attention should be devoted to etudes as to the pieces which succeed them. In the incomparable studies of Czerny and Clementi, etc., many marks of expression can be added to those already given for aid in the performance, so that these etudes afford not only the best opportunity possible for cultivating the hand, but serve as the best possible preparation for the development of musical taste in the pieces one may have in course of preparation. Like the piece, the etude must be divided into phrases learned by heart, and the fingering be carefully considered. It is undeniable that the choice of the latter depends on the conformation of the hands. Instead of being unalterable the fingering must sometimes change to suit a given tempo; it is best to make use of the most difficult fingering for etudes and the easiest for pieces.

It is invaluable that one practise at first each hand separately and later both together. By occasionally making use of the metronome, slow time can be gradually increased in speed until it reaches the exact tempo prescribed. That which has sounded excellent in slow time will not lose its good qualities by an unspoiled and gradual transition into quick time; only an immediate change from slow to quick would endanger the carefully acquired correctness of form, so creating a lamentable result. In order to attain great precision and clearness in playing, the student should attempt, after having mastered the correct position and movement of the hand, to practise difficult passages without looking at the keyboard. The study of etudes as well as that of pieces must be subjected to the sharpest self-criticism, which criticism can only be successfully applied by the pianist, when he interrupts his playing over and over again to re-think the passage played. In the pauses which thus ensue he will be able to call up before his mind that which he has already played, paying attentive heed to what has sounded, and as has already been said before, regarding the use of the pedal, the correct and incorrect will re-sound in his memory, thus assisting him in bringing the whole to perfection. This inward listening of the player marks an important achievement, for it not only increases immensely his sense of rhythm, use of the pedal and gradation of sound, but it also sharpens his memory, impressing firmly upon it the actual image of the notes. Besides, an habitual absorption in the task in hand protects the mind against a paralyzing nervousness when playing before an audience, be it public or private. Finally, the student should not forget, when studying a piece,

Es hat dies einen bestimmten Zweck: der Spieler soll das erforderliche Vertrauen zu sich gewinnen, bei Gelegenheit des Vorspielens sein Können momentan zur Geltung zu bringen und nicht der Sklave jedesmaligen vorbereitenden Uebens werden. Da aber kein Studientag ohne technische Uebungen vergehen sollte, so möge man sie auf den Schluss des Tagewerkes verlegen.

Um auf das Studium der Etuden zurückzukommen, so sei demselben die gleiche Aufmerksamkeit wie dem der darauffolgenden Stücke gewidmet. In die unübertrefflichen Uebungswerke von Czerny, Clementi u. s. w. lassen sich zu den bereits bestehenden vielen Vortragszeichen noch manche andere hinzufügen, so dass diese Etuden nicht nur für die Ausbildung der Hand das Ausgezeichnetste leisten, sondern auch für die Entfaltung des musikalischen Geschmackes in den eigentlichen Vortragsstücken vorbereitend wirken können. Sowie das Stück, muss auch die Etude phrasiert, auswendig gelernt und der Fingersatz wohl überlegt werden. Dass dessen Wahl vom Bau der Hände abhängt und trotz genauer Festsetzung manchmal durch Veränderung des Tempos eine Mitveränderung erfahren muss, ist zweifellos; ebenso dass für Etuden der schwierigste, für Stücke der leichteste Fingersatz anzuwenden ist.

Weiter ist zu fordern, dass zuerst jede Hand *allein*, später beide Hände zusammen geübt werden. Unter zeitweiligem Mitschlagen des Metronoms wird aus dem langsamen in das richtige, vorgeschriebene Tempo vorwärts geschritten. Was im langsamen Tempo vorzüglich geklungen hat, wird bei vorsichtigem Uebergang in das schnelle Tempo an Güte nichts einbüssen; nur ein unvermittelt jäher Stoss würde die Sache gefährden und müsste ein ungünstiges Resultat herbeiführen. Zur Erlangung grosser Sicherheit und Reinheit des Spieles versuche man, wenn man die richtige Haltung und Bewegungen der Hand bereits inne hat, schwere Stellen, ohne auf die Tastatur zu blicken, zu üben. Das Studium der Etuden muss ebenso wie das der Stücke der *schärfsten Selbstkritik* unterworfen werden, die von dem Spieler nur dann mit Erfolg ausgeübt wird, wenn er sein Spiel immer wieder unterbricht. In der dadurch entstandenen Pause wird er sich das soeben Gespielte geistig vergegenwärtigen können, demselben gespannt nachhorchen und wie früher schon gelegentlich des Pedalisierens erwähnt wurde, wird ihm in der Erinnerung Richtiges und Unrichtiges nachklingen und letzteres zur Vervollkommnung anregen. *Dieses innerliche Zuhören* des Spielers bedeutet eine wichtige Errungenschaft; nicht nur, dass es seine Empfindung für Rhythmus, Pedalisierung und Klangfarbe auf das Aeusserste steigert, es schärft auch sein Gedächtnis, dem sich das Notenbild fest einprägt. Auch in Bezug auf das Spielen in Gesell-

to play it over two or three times to begin with, in order to gather the musical value, form an impression of the whole and prepare a plan for its proper performance. This prelude is followed by the detailed study of everything already discussed; the résumé of these includes attention to hand position, choice of fingering, correct rhythm and use of the pedal, pauses, inward listening, criticism, and finally the repeated playing of the whole with the detected defects corrected.

As regards learning by heart,—which power develops of itself through inward listening coupled with the imprinting on the mind the image of the notes,—it is advisable, as a test of memory, to go through the piece mentally only, without looking at the music and without a piano. Besides this the student should question himself as to the exact notes forming some particular bar in a difficult passage, for instance the fourth or the sixth, or some other, and having picked it out from the rest, should, after mentally reviewing it, try to play it exactly on the piano, or name the notes to himself in their proper sequence. The same thing can be done with starting at some particular part of a bar. In this sort of testing, the student should take care to begin with the correct fingering, correct pedal as well as correct accent. This method of studying, though apparently tedious and troublesome, is the shortest path to a lasting intellectual possession of musical works, for even after laying them aside for a long while, the briefest repetition is sufficient to enable the pianist to render them with certainty.

CHAPTER VI.

THE DEEPENING OF MUSICAL CULTURE.

Although the playing of the piano does not demand an absolutely musical ear, still it is necessary to cultivate the latter as much as possible. Methodical and regular training can do much to accomplish this. It is quite sufficient to set aside for this purpose only a small amount of time daily. In the beginning one should study simple intervals within the scope of an octave, studying afterward the sound of one note played in conjunction with another, following this with chords and combinations of chords until finally one can write down chorals and other short pieces from hearing them only.

Reading at sight must also not be neglected, taking for granted that the hand and finger movements are

schaft und Oeffentlichkeit bewirkt die gewohnte Vertiefung in die Aufgabe eine Ablenkung von der oft lähmenden Idee des Vorspielens. Schliesslich vergesse man nicht das Einstudieren von Stücken mit zwei- bis dreimaligem Durchspielen zu beginnen, um aus dem Gesamteindruck den musikalischen Wert zu erfassen und für deren Vortrag eine Skizze zu entwerfen. Diesem Eingang folgt das Detailstudium mit allem bereits Besprochenen, das Résumé der Anwendung von Handstellung und Fingersatzwahl, von rhythmischen und Pedalisierungs-Vorteilen, vom Pausieren, innerlichen Zuhören, Kritisieren und endlich mehrmaligen Vorspielen mit Verbesserung der bei diesen Gelegenheiten noch sich zeigenden Mängel.

In Betreff des *Auswendiglernens*, das sich bei dem innerlichen Zuhorchen durch gleichzeitiges Aufnehmen des Notenbildes von selbst ergiebt, empfiehlt es sich ferner zur Prüfung des Gedächtnisses, das Stück nur im Geiste, ohne Anschauen des Notenblattes und ohne Klavier, durchzunehmen. Ausserdem befrage man sich um irgend einen Takt aus einer schweren Stelle, z. B. um den 4., den 6., oder sonst einen, und versuche ihn dann gesondert von den vorherigen, nachdem man diese im Geiste passiert hat, präzise auf dem Klavier zu spielen oder sich die Töne desselben in ihrer Reihenfolge zu nennen. In gleicher Weise kann man mit den Taktteilen vorgehen. Bei Spielen des betreffenden Taktes und Taktteiles setze man mit dem richtigen Fingersatz, richtigen Pedal und richtigen Accent ein. Diese Art des Studierens, welche langwierig und mühsam erscheint, ist der kürzeste Weg zu dauerndem geistigen Besitz der musikalischen Werke, denn selbst nach langem Ruhenlassen derselben genügt die geringste Wiederholung zur Befähigung einer sicheren Wiedergabe.

KAPITEL VI.

DIE ERWEITERUNG DER MUSIKALISCHEN BILDUNG.

Obgleich die Behandlung des Klavieres den Besitz des absoluten musikalischen Gehörs nicht erfordert, so ist es doch notwendig, das Gehör so viel als möglich auszubilden. Zu dessen Vervollkommnung vermag eine regelrechte und regelmässige Schulung viel beizutragen. Es genügt derselben eine ganz kurze Spanne Zeit im Tage einzuräumen. Vor allem anderen nehme man das Studium der Intervallschritte in engster Begrenzung, also innerhalb einer Oktave vor, studiere dann den Zusammenklang derselben, darauf Accorde und Accordverbindungen, bis man endlich Choräle und andere kurze Stücke nach dem Gehör niederschreiben kann. Ebenso vernachlässige man nicht das Blattlesen. Die Sicherheit der Hand- und Fingerbewe-

already correct. At the first reading through of a piece, one should attempt to express its special characteristics, to apply the pedal properly and to go through the piece to the end in approximately correct time without stopping, in spite of mistakes and note omissions. In doing this the student must enlighten himself as to which are the difficult passages without, however, practising them, and should afterward repeat the reading, with an increase of speed. At first the student should choose pieces below the level of his musical abilities in order to give his eye the chance of reading ahead, not to be obliged to keep it fixed on one point because of a number of big chords. Without losing the time it would necessarily take to look at the keyboard, the fingers must strike the unfamiliar distances as well and as correctly as possible, which will not be difficult if his method of study has been correct. In addition to this, transposing into other keys cultivates a musical ear.

An excellent preliminary study for fully understanding great orchestral performances in concert halls—with their stimulating after-effect on the comprehension and performance of every disciple of music and therefore also of the pianist—is the playing of duets on either one or two pianos, of various works, most of which are so excellently arranged for the purpose. By playing at sight with another, the reader will be compelled to sharpen his sense of rhythm and to make his ear exercise a still sterner watchfulness as to harmonies and the use of the pedal. In the same way chamber music, which comprises some of the most precious gems of piano literature, played in company with other instruments, is highly to be recommended for the deepening of musical culture; for the subordinating of the separate parts to one common object is one of the best means for the promotion of the above. Equally indispensable is the study of harmony, counterpoint and different forms of composition, for this study is the most valuable aid toward correct phrasing.

gungen wird vorausgesetzt. Man bemühe sich schon bei dem erstmaligen Durchlesen eines Stückes das Charakteristische im Ausdruck zu treffen, gutes Pedal anzuwenden und das Stück ziemlich annähernd an das richtige Tempo ohne Unterbrechung, selbst bei Unterlaufen von Notenfehlern oder Weglassen mancher Noten, bis an das Ende durchzuführen. Hierauf erkläre man sich schwierige Stellen, ohne sie jedoch zu üben und wiederhole das Lesen mit Steigerung des Tempos. Es ist ratsam, zuerst Stücke unter dem Niveau des musikalischen Könnens zu wählen, um das Auge an das rasche Vorwärtsschauen zu gewöhnen und dasselbe nicht durch die Auftürmung komplizierter Accorde an einem Punkte festzubannen. Ohne die Zeit mit Schauen auf die Tastatur zu verlieren, müssen die Finger möglichst geschickt die ihnen fremden Distanzen greifen, was ihnen jedoch von der Art guten Studierens her kein neuer Vorgang ist. Auch das Transponieren in andere Tonarten macht musikalisch.

Ein ausgezeichnetes Vorstudium für das Verständnis der grossen Orchesteraufführungen im Konzertsaale mit ihrer anregenden Rückwirkung auf Auffassung und Ausführung jedes Musiktreibenden, also auch des Pianisten, ist das Vierhändigspielen auf einem oder zwei Klavieren der zu diesem Zwecke meist so ausgezeichnet arrangierten Werke. Der vom Blatt Lesende wird durch das Zusammenspiel gezwungen, sein rhythmisches Gefühl noch mehr zu schärfen, sein Ohr noch strengere Kritik über Harmonien und Pedalisierung üben zu lassen. Desgleichen ist das Ensemblespiel mit anderen Instrumenten in Form von Duos, Trios, etc., das überdies die kostbarsten Perlen der Musikliteratur umfasst, für die Erweiterung der musikalischen Bildung höchst empfehlenswert und die Unterordnung des Einzelnen unter den gemeinsamen Zweck eines der förderndsten Mittel. Geradezu unerlässlich ist das Studium der Harmonielehre, des Kontrapunktes und der Formenlehre, das der Phrasierung die wertvollsten Hilfsmittel darbietet.

CONCLUDING REMARKS.

We have now reached the end of our book, the finale of which forms a link with the introduction. In order to be able to absorb himself in the imperishable treasures of pianoforte literature, to enter with a full and entire perception into their changeful character of seriousness and humor, their passionate and tender shades, the disciple of music must have already made himself master of all technical difficulties. He who wishes to begin perfecting his technique through the finest compositions of Beethoven, Schumann, and the other great composers, would find himself on the wrong path, and so will he who considers it sufficient to learn thoroughly by painstaking study one single piece by these great masters. Only he who has studied these works in their entirety can possibly acquire the necessary intellectual understanding of the great masters and enter into and reproduce their special characteristics.

As to execution, much may certainly be achieved by industry and exact work; interpretation can be developed to a high degree by the advantages of a fine touch, assured rhythm, and fine use of the pedal, all assisted and supported by musical culture; but to the highest point of spiritual and intellectual grasp only he can attain who is chosen by nature to be so great and worthy.

SCHLUSSBEMERKUNGEN.

Wir stehen am Ende unseres Buches. Sein Finale knüpfe an die Ouverture an: *Um sich in die unvergänglichen Schätze der Klavierliteratur versenken, ihrem wechselvollen Charakter von Ernst und Humor, ihren leidenschaftlichen und zarten Stimmungen mit ungeteilter Empfindung hingeben zu können, muss der Kunstjünger bereits Herr der technischen Schwierigkeiten geworden sein.* Wer bei Beethoven'schen, Schumann'schen und anderen Kompositionen klassischen Gepräges erst Technik erlangen wollte, befände sich auf einem Irrwege; ebenso jener, dem es genügend erscheinen würde, vereinzelt dieses oder jenes Tonstück unserer grossen Meister sich in genauerem Studium zu eigen zu machen. Nur wer diese Werke in ihrer Gesamtheit studiert hat, kann die nötigen geistigen Beziehungen zu deren Schöpfern gewinnen und den jedem eigentümlichen Charakter erfassen und wiedergeben.

In Betreff des Vortrags lässt sich durch Fleiss und genaue Arbeit gewiss viel erreichen; durch die Vorzüge eines schönen Anschlages, gefestigten Rhythmus', feiner Pedalisierung, durch musikalische Bildung unterstützt, kann sich die Wiedergabe zu bedeutender Höhe entwickeln; zur höchsten Stufe der geistigen Auffassung jedoch gelangt nur das angeborene, auserwählte **Talent.**